How DBT Helped Me:

Prior to visiting Lilac Center and starting Dialectical Behavior Therapy (DBT), my life was a mess. But as I learned DBT skills, my life began to change. I am now able to safely express my emotions without the fear of rejection. I use the DBT skills on a daily basis. I am thankful to Lilac Center for showing me a more enjoyable way of life.
-**Karrie G.**

I was so disconnected from my own emotions that I did not notice the hopelessness that had utterly consumed me. My only feeling was that I was unbearably tired and suicide seemed to be the only possible relief. It has been nearly four years since I began Dialectical Behavior Therapy (DBT). The self-awareness and relational skills it teaches have given me clarity beyond what I thought achievable. I am able to take hold of my mind and bring myself peace. I have learned to successfully navigate relationships of every kind. DBT has not only saved my life, it has given me a healthier, more fulfilled life to live.
- **Joshua M.**

Throughout my life, attempts to find relief from the emotional anguish I felt internally had been met with very little progress. My relationships were constantly in turmoil. I was continually looking for reassurance because I was convinced the people in my life were going to abandon me. My way of obtaining that reassurance was destructive and deflating the relationships, making things worse. DBT is something useful that has helped me keep and strengthen my relationships. It has provided me with skills to help me tolerate intense emotions that were causing extreme suffering and hopelessness. Using the skills offered in this workbook has given me a different and more effective way to navigate through life, increasing my sense of hope and self-respect. Challenges will always arise, but the quality of my life has significantly improved since I started utilizing DBT.
- **Marcie M.**

I'm grateful for Amy Tibbitts and the Lilac Center. I learned DBT Skills through Amy's loving compassion and patience and finally I felt validated for the first time. It took me a long time to learn that I'm not going to get what I need through self-harming behaviors and I was tired of making up stories and lies. My hope is that others will find a compassionate therapist who can teach them these skills. It has really made a difference in my life. One encouraging word is priceless when all feels lost. Open your world to the endless possibilities healthy living can bring you!
- **Angie K.**

Amy is one of the most caring people I have ever met, and the Lilac Center is the very essence of a safe place for adults and adolescents who struggle with mental health issues. Borderline Personality Disorder can be a complex and insidious foe, but Amy and her Lilac Center colleagues keep it from being a terminal condition for many people. Dialectical Behavior Therapy provides the solid base of skills fundamentals, problem-solving strategies, and personal support that those who suffer from BPD need in order to transition from their chaotic existences to a normal, centered life. The ideas and methods outlined in the following pages do work, are quite effective, and it is my wish that they are as transformative for your life as they have been for mine.
- **Allen L.**

When I was strategically planning what I was going to wear for the day based on what types of watches, bracelets or colors I could use for covering self-harm injuries, I realized that the recommendation that my doctor had been giving me to seek care at the Lilac Center might not be such a bad idea. I had been self-injuring for quite some time and that was always his answer: "The Lilac Center." It is now my answer as well. Since coming here, I have never looked back! DBT is providing me with the help I need to become stronger and create positive change in my life!
- **Jen A.**

THIS WORKBOOK BELONGS TO:

....

A DBT SKILLS WORKBOOK

YOU UNTANGLED

PRACTICAL TOOLS TO MANAGE YOUR EMOTIONS AND IMPROVE YOUR LIFE

AMY TIBBITTS, MSW, LCSW

ISBN: 978-0-9898021-0-9
Copyright © 2014 Amy Tibbitts, MSW, LCSW

All rights reserved. No part of this book shall be reproduced, stored in a retrieval system, or transmitted by any means—electronic, mechanical, photocopying, recording, or otherwise—without written permission from the publisher, except for the inclusion of brief quotations in a review.

Every effort has been made to make this book as complete and as accurate as possible, but no warranty of fitness is implied. The information is provided on an as-is basis. The authors and the publisher shall have neither liability nor responsibility to any person or entity with respect to any loss or damages arising from the information contained in this book. We encourage you to seek help from professionals in your local area.

Dedication

To my husband,
Tony, you are my best friend and your partnership, love, acceptance and support have always transformed any darkness in my life into pure light. Thank you for designing this workbook.
Your talent continues to astound me.

To my children,
Townsend, when you were born, I was filled with so much love that my heart grew in ways I didn't know were possible. And Novella, the moment you were born, all that love was returned directly to me — giving me the strength to love myself.

To my sister-in-law,
Rachael, your words come together like magic!
Thank you for editing this book.

To all my clients —
the ones who have found a life worth living and
to those who are still struggling — thank you for walking with me down this path toward healing and for sharing your personal truths and wisdom.

Table of Contents

FORWARD: FINDING GREATNESS BEHIND MADNESS 1
USING THIS WORKBOOK 4

chapter 1:
WHAT IS BORDERLINE PERSONALITY DISORDER? 7
chapter 2:
WHAT IS DIALECTICAL BEHAVIOR THERAPY? 20
chapter 3:
DBT: THE KEY CONCEPTS 23
chapter 4:
SELF-ASSESSMENT TOOLS FOR BPD 29
chapter 5:
GETTING TO WISE MIND 43
chapter 6:
CRISIS SURVIVAL SKILLS 64
chapter 7:
HOW EMOTIONS WORK 86
chapter 8:
SO, WHAT GOOD ARE EMOTIONS ANYWAY? 104
chapter 9:
SECONDARY EMOTIONS 109
chapter 10:
SPECTRUMS OF EMOTIONS 115
chapter 11:
EMOTIONAL TOLERANCE 123
chapter 12:
FINDING YOUR PURPOSE 139
chapter 13:
MAINTAINING HEALTHY RELATIONSHIPS 144

CONCLUSION 176

quick find: Worksheets and Excercises

chapter 1: What Is Borderline Personality Disorder?
BORDERLINE PERSONALITY DISORDER QUICK TEST............ 9
COMMIT TO LIFE CONTRACT 11
THE UNSTABLE 5................. 13

chapter 4: Self-Assessment Tools for BPD
ASSESSING YOUR EMOTIONS 31
ASSESSING YOUR BEHAVIORS.................. 33
ASSESSING YOUR RELATIONSHIPS 35
ASSESSING YOUR THOUGHTS 37
ASSESSING YOUR SENSE OF SELF................ 39

chapter 5: Getting To Wise Mind
MINDFULNESS EXERCISES.................. 50
AWARENESS AND ATTENTION TO YOUR ENVIRONMENT........53
STATES OF MIND: BE MINDFUL 56
GETTING INTO WISE MIND 57
MINDFULNESS "WHAT" SKILLS 59
MINDFULNESS "HOW" SKILLS................ 61
RECOGNIZING DIALECTICAL DILEMMAS 63

chapter 6: Crisis Survival Skills
GETTING READY: AN EXERCISE FOR PREPARATION 67
NEXT STEPS: PREPARING FOR CRISIS................75
CRISIS SURVIVAL.................. 77
POST-CRISIS ASSESSMENT................ 79
IN-THE-MOMENT GUIDE 81
TAKING ACTION IN THE MOMENT 83
SELF SOOTHE: "5 SENSES" SKILL................ 86
MAKE IMPROVEMENT EVERY DAY: "IMPROVE" 88
CRISIS SURVIVAL SKILLS: "ACCEPTS" 90
LISTING PROS AND CONS 92

chapter 7: How Emotions Work
YOUR EMOTIONAL HERITAGE................ 95
EXPLORING YOUR BELIEFS ABOUT EMOTIONS 96

chapter 9: Secondary Emotions
YOUR EXPERIENCE OF SECONDARY EMOTIONS................ 111
EMOTION SKILL: MINDFULNESS TO YOUR EMOTIONS 113

chapter 10: Spectrums Of Emotions
EMOTION SPECTRUM CHEAT SHEET................ 116
AWARENESS TO THE 5 COMPONENTS................ 117
EMPHASIZING DESCRIBING................ 119
ASSESSING YOUR PRACTICE 121
DAILY SITUATIONS FOR NOTICING EMOTIONS 122

chapter 11: Emotional Tolerance
TOLERATING EMOTIONS: BEGINNING PRACTICE................ 126
TOLERATING EMOTIONS: MORE EXPOSURE 128
BIOLOGICAL FACTORS VS. SOCIAL FACTORS 132
CHANGING EMOTIONS BY ACTING OPPOSITE 133
THOUGHTS AND BEHAVIORS: SADNESS 134
THOUGHTS AND BEHAVIORS: FEAR................ 135
THOUGHTS AND BEHAVIORS: SHAME 136
THOUGHTS AND BEHAVIORS: ANGER................ 137
THOUGHTS AND BEHAVIORS: JOY................ 138

chapter 12: Finding Your Purpose
BE EMOTIONALLY PROACTIVE: PLAN AHEAD TO COPE 142

chapter 13: Maintaining Healthy Relationships
DISCOVER THE FUTURE. FIND HAPPINESS AND JOY........... 145
HOW TO CREATE HEALTHY RELATIONSHIPS................ 149
THINGS YOU HOLD VALUABLE VS. DEMANDS 165
BALANCING WANTS AND SHOULDS 167
PRIORITIES VS. DEMANDS................ 168
REDUCING VULNERABILITY: "MEETS MASTERY" SKILL........ 169
GET WHAT YOU WANT: "SPEAK UP" SKILL................ 170
CULTIVATE GOOD RELATIONSHIPS: "RELAX" SKILL............. 172
KEEP YOUR SELF-RESPECT: "WORTH" SKILL................ 174

DISCLAIMER

This book is meant as a resource to help you learn about Dialectical Behavior Therapy and skills to help with Borderline Personality Disorder. This book is not a replacement for diagnosis and treatment from a professional licensed Therapist. We encourage you to seek out professional help and attend individual and group therapy from a DBT provider.

THE LILAC CENTER: *who we are*

Kansas City, Mo.,-based Lilac Center is the premier provider of DBT services in the greater Kansas City metro and surrounding area.

For over 10 years, the Lilac Center has successfully provided a wide range of psychological services with a Dialectical Behavior Therapy (DBT) focus. DBT teaches problem-solving techniques designed to foster a healthy balance in thoughts, feelings and actions.

This workbook was developed by Amy Tibbitts, director of the Lilac Center, and has been used in treating our clients for years. After continuing to refine and improve it, we decided to share this useful tool with others looking for information and help using DBT.

In addition, we have developed a companion website: *mydbtgroup.com* that includes actual videos of group sessions of Amy teaching the skills found in this book. The website also includes worksheets and additional resources about Borderline Personality Disorder and Dialectical Behavior Therapy. Many of our clients have found *mydbtgroup.com* to be very helpful in learning DBT and better understanding the skills in this book. We hope you will too.

mydbtgroup.com /YOUUNTANGLED

- www.lilaccenter.org
- www.mydbtgroup.com
- facebook.com/lilaccenter
- @lilaccenter

ACKNOWLEDGMENTS

First and foremost, I must thank Marsha Linehan, Ph.D., for her pioneering spirit and groundbreaking techniques in psychological therapy. This workbook would not be possible without her immeasurable influence. By introducing the theory of Dialectical Behavior Therapy in 1991 and eventually publicly revealing her own personal struggles, Linehan has provided a framework of hope for so many people who suffer from emotion dysregulation. I am grateful for Linehan's teachings and continue to be inspired by the precedent she has set.

forward
FINDING GREATNESS BEHIND MADNESS

By Amy Tibbitts, MSW, LCSW

Back in 2004, I was watching the 46th annual Grammy Awards and a quote was relayed from George Harrison that caught my attention.

In Harrison's words, after his initial visit to the United States, he recalled the Beatles questioning, "America has everything, why should they want us?"

Yet the Beatles changed music forever. However, it is clear from his comment that even George Harrison seemed to experience self-doubt.

It is refreshing to relate with the rare humility of a superstar. Many of my clients have said something similar, believing they have nothing to offer and that they are only a burden to this world.

Clients whom I see with Borderline Personality Disorder (BPD) live in a realm darkened by fears of inadequacy. They are continually tormented by self-doubt.

When providing treatment, I am often frustrated because I can see the potential greatness behind the insecurity. And yet my frustration pales in comparison to the heartbreak that family and friends endure as they love and support the individual who is mentally suffering.

Dialectical Behavior Therapy (DBT) offers a comprehensive and compassionate approach to treating Borderline Personality Disorder.

I can endlessly describe the clinical problems people with BPD face. Suicidal tendencies, self-harm, chaotic relationships, eating disorders, substance abuse, financial problems, sexual promiscuity, etc., are among some of the major problems.

I cannot, however, find the words for the pain and suffering carried by these individuals.

When a client of mine commits to living, I know that it will be a true challenge for the client to endure. The sadness in the thought that life is so unbearable — and that death makes the most sense — is hopefully something most people might never have to understand.

For those who can understand, they should give DBT a chance. It requires a leap of faith, but so does death.

I have provided DBT on an out-patient basis for the past 13 years. I have contracted with many major managed care companies to provide a comprehensive model of therapy based on Marsha Linehan's renowned clinical work and research. Overall, the results have been outstanding and it has been truly rewarding to witness — firsthand — transformations in the lives of my clients.

The major areas in which I have seen marked improvement are a reduction in para-suicidal behaviors, increased willingness and compliance for treatment (i.e. taking medication as prescribed), following through with skills attainment, improved self-care, reduction in reckless behaviors and substance abuse, improved relationships, improved self-image and balanced eating.

Results have been especially extraordinary with many of my clients who have co-occurring eating disorder.

Often these individuals fluctuate between overeating, binging and purging, and restricting. The therapy has been effective in helping these individuals find balance with food. Many have been able to reduce their overeating and many of the extremely overweight people have actually lost significant amounts of weight.

Those who restrict and/or binge and purge have been able to maintain a healthy weight. The changes were so dramatic for some that if "before and after" pictures had been taken, I could successfully advertise like Bill Phillips does for his "Body for LIFE" program! Focusing on mindful eating, several of my clients lost over 20 pounds, with some clients losing 80-plus pounds.

The cost savings surrounding the 30 members then enrolled in the DBT program referred by a major managed care company were significant. In the year prior to undergoing DBT, the 30 members used 281 acute in-patient hospital days. The following year, after joining the DBT program, these same clients used only 5 in-patient hospital days.

But it's important to realize that outcome measurement is so much more than simply a dollar figure; the DBT process results in tremendous fringe benefits.

Society must learn to value the intangible benefits of eliminating human distress and improving a person's quality of life. In doing so, society as a whole will realize benefits that include, but are not limited to, the tax advantages of an individual's ability to return to work; children again being cared for by their parents; decreased calls to emergency personnel, etc. Not to mention the overwhelming personal benefits for individuals who have been defined as mentally ill who are now moving toward self-reliance.

There is a growing need for mental health professionals to define and explain to private managed care companies the extensive benefits associated with providing longer-term care that may exceed an individual's policy and would fall outside the boundaries of "treatment as usual." I believe treatment should be provided to individuals based on the research that defines best practice, not a predetermined dollar amount that an insurance company sets. Through defining and researching best practices, I also believe the treatment provided will ultimately be the most cost-effective. There is room to assist individuals in getting their mental health needs met within the private sector. If people are able to maintain their jobs and utilize their health insurance to address their mental health needs, everyone benefits in the big picture.

There is also an immeasurable intrinsic value because, in the long run, these once emotionally-tormented souls can again find meaning in life.

I truly believe that DBT is invaluable when it comes to how it can assist clients in defining and achieving their own personal goals and setting a new standard for life.

USING THIS WORKBOOK

You're reading this workbook most likely because you have been diagnosed by a mental health professional, through assessment, or you have been having difficulties in important areas of your life with your mood, your emotions and relationships.

Perhaps you've done some research and wonder if Borderline Personality Disorder (BPD) fits as a description of the problems you've been facing.

You may even be in treatment with a therapist who is treating you for BPD, perhaps someone trained in Dialectical Behavior Therapy (DBT), or another therapist who works with a different theoretical orientation. Or you may be using this workbook as an adjunctive part to your Web-based therapy though **mydbtgroup.com**. If you're not aware of this website, it is a great resource for videos, worksheets and additional info about Dialectical Behavior Therapy and Borderline Personality Disorder. You will see highlighted areas throughout the book that guide you to additional resources on **mydbtgroup.com**. Our basic membership is free for those who have purchased the book. Enter "youuntangled" at checkout.

Whatever the path that led you here, this workbook can help you.

EXPLORING BPD

BPD develops as a response to biological vulnerabilities in addition to adverse life events.

In this workbook, we will explore your *past, present* and *future*.

Initially, you will work on managing the symptoms associated with Borderline Personality Disorder. The most important thing is **safety and stability**, so we will start with the present, and developing DBT skills.

Then we will delve deeply into emotion recognition, acceptance and control. These components make up the core foundation of DBT.

Ultimately, you will work on building a life worth living; a life in which you are connected, grounded and able to live congruently with your values and participate fully in life as it happens.

HOW CAN THIS BOOK HELP ME?

Whether you are working through this book alone, or with a therapist as part of your treatment, we hope that you will find the principles and exercises clear and practical.

This may be your first exposure to Dialectical Behavior Therapy in a workbook format. To reap the benefit of authentic DBT, it's best if you're working with professionals who are trained in the model and who can provide individual DBT therapy sessions, as well as DBT skills training group.

That's not always possible, of course, so the next best option, in our opinion, is to work with therapists who can provide DBT-informed treatment and who are willing to help you apply these skills as well as adopt the assumptions and principles of DBT while you are in treatment with them.

If you are currently without access to a mental health treatment provider, you can still benefit greatly from this workbook, particularly as you determine to stay the course of practice. Commit to yourself to learn and apply the exercises, and you will find yourself increasing mastery over your behaviors, tolerating strong emotions, and improving relationships.

You will be able to observe the past without getting swept up by it, and you will recognize the impact it has on your current life. This workbook will provide you not just concepts, but practical tools that you can apply immediately to your situation. You will begin to make important changes so that you can gain more control over yourself and begin to thrive in the long-term.

BREAK FREE

The clients we have seen with Borderline Personality Disorder have broken free of mental restraints, overcome life-threatening behaviors and self-harm, greatly improved their relationships, and have cultivated lifestyles that are closer to what they have always wanted for themselves.

There are no guarantees for healing or cure from intense emotional sensitivity, or from the inevitable pain you will face in life, but there is a hope that you will learn to relate with all of this in a new manner using a new set of skills to adapt and respond in ways that are effective for staying on the path you choose for your life.

Understand up front, there are no easy solutions in this workbook. But this book does offer hope for change made possible through the committed application of DBT principles and practices, the reality of changed lives, and existing research data that supports the effectiveness of DBT.

Start living the *tomorrow* you've always envisioned *today*.

THE FUTURE IS A BRIGHT ONE.
If you are suffering, there is always hope.

Things can and *do get better.*

Chapter I

WHAT IS BORDERLINE PERSONALITY DISORDER?

Borderline Personality Disorder (BPD) is a very serious disorder with many serious consequences for those who suffer with the disorder. I believe Borderline Personality Disorder is a response to pervasive trauma. For individuals who are suffering, you may have developed maladaptive coping to abusive environments. The behaviors that are now destroying you may have once helped you survive an impossible situation.

80%

Approximately 80 percent of all people diagnosed with BPD have a history of at least one **serious suicide attempt.**

❌ It is estimated that about the same number have engaged in at least one episode of non-lethal self-harm, or what professionals refer to as parasuicidal behaviors, and it is estimated that 10 percent of these persons complete suicide.

AMONG THE PERSONALITY DISORDERS, BPD IS THE MOST-ASSOCIATED WITH SUICIDE.

HOWEVER, as you will find in the pages of this workbook, great change can be accomplished in overcoming many of these problems as you learn critical concepts and principles, practice them diligently, and ultimately orient yourself toward a more healthy and effective way of living.

It is sometimes an appropriate response to reality to go insane.

Philip K. Dick

Borderline Personality Disorder *quick test!*

DO YOU EXPERIENCE ANY OF THESE?

- ☐ I usually disregard my own preferences in order to please other people.
- ☐ I tend to jump from job to job and from one interest to another.
- ☐ I feel empty inside, or like there is a hole inside of me.
- ☐ I tend to copy or emulate the style of other people.
- ☐ I need other people to tell me how I'm doing in most areas of life.
- ☐ I try to be or do what other people want me to be or do.
- ☐ I often feel disconnected from the world.
- ☐ I rarely know what I want from myself or others.
- ☐ I often feel numb or don't feel anything.
- ☐ I'm easily influenced by the opinions of others.
- ☐ After completing activities or driving, I don't recall doing it.
- ☐ I frequently feel like I'm in a dreamy fog.
- ☐ Even as an adult, I don't know what I want to do with my life.
- ☐ I have on several occasions been in physical fights.
- ☐ I don't have a consistent dress style, education or work experience.

The skills taught in DBT can help you overcome your emotional turmoil.

step 1

Make a commitment to LIVE.

✏️ **Exercise:**
Write out your commitment and share it with a close loved one. If you are isolated, write it and post it in a visible spot. Love yourself enough to give this process an opportunity.

commit to life CONTRACT

I _____ on this day _____

I commit to be kind to myself and I choose to live.

I will commit myself to learning skills that will help me regulate my emotions and become a healthier person.

I will embrace positive thoughts.

I know it won't be easy and I may have days that I struggle.

I ask for patience in return.

I know that I am loved.

I deserve happiness.

I have a purpose.

I commit to life.

_____

signed

Borderline Personality Disorder, as conceptualized in the framework of Dialectical Behavior Therapy (DBT), is understood as primarily a disorder of emotional responses that spills over into other important areas of life, including behaviors, relationships, thought patterns and relationship to self.

For individuals who are able to handle their emotions in a healthy productive way, he or she validates the emotion and then works with the emotional energy to create the change wanted in his or her life, and hence is able to reduce emotional distress.

For individuals who struggle with BPD, frequently he or she tries to control the emotion, invalidating the internal feeling and then behaviorally tries to get rid of the emotion by some impulsive response, such as:

- ☑ self-harm

- ☑ substance abuse

- ☑ eating-disordered behavior

- ☑ gambling

- ☑ impulsive spending

- ☑ reckless driving

- ☑ hair pulling

- ☑ sexually acting out, etc.

Following the impulsive denial of the validity of your own emotional state, the invalidated emotion will temporarily change in response to the impulsive behavior. However, it will return even more intensely. Often individuals find themselves in an addictive process feeling more compelled to repeat the harmful behavior due to the intensity of emotional urges.

The Unstable 5

The following five areas frequently present as the most unstable and often are mired in consistent patterns of negative behavior over a period of years, bringing unimaginable chaos into the life of the person with BPD as well as into the lives of their friends and family.

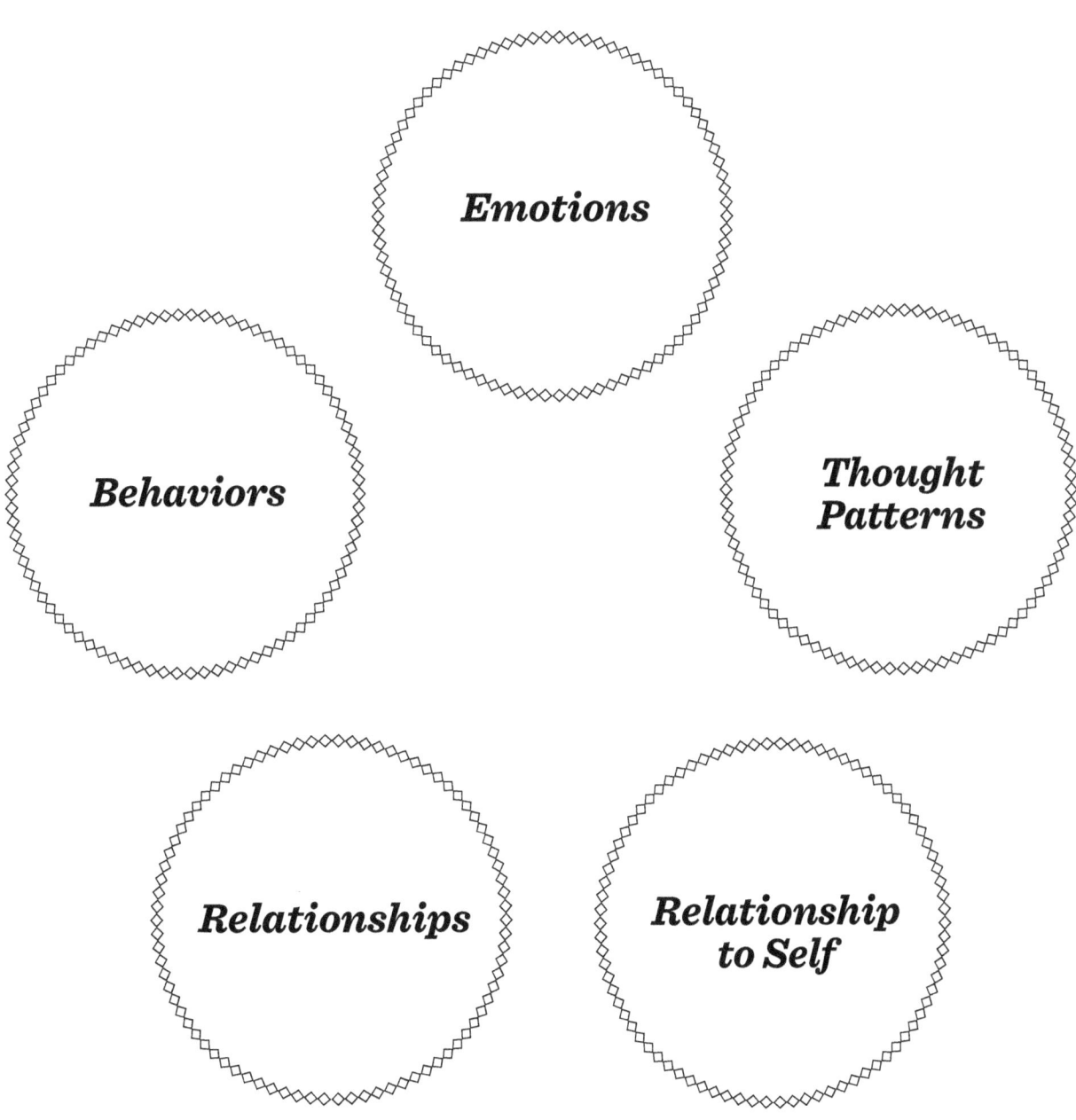

WHAT IS BORDERLINE PERSONALITY DISORDER?

✏️ Exercise:
The Unstable 5

Unpack these five areas and list the harmful ways you invalidate or believe harm has been created in these areas.

Emotions:
....
....
....
....
....

Behaviors:
....
....
....
....
....

Relationships:
....
....
....
....
....

Thought Patterns:
....
....
....
....
....

Relationship to Self:
....
....
....
....

⊙ The Unstable 5: **Emotions**

DBT conceptualizes BPD to be primarily a disorder of **emotion regulation**. People with BPD experience chronic negative emotional states such as anxiety, sadness, irritability and anger, also demonstrating difficulty with the expression of anger.

This means two things. On the one hand, people with BPD will often mask their anger over controlling it, not expressing it even when anger expression would be appropriate. For many of these people, there is a fear and anxiety that by expressing anger they may become entirely explosive. And so they try to control their anger — a skill all people need — to an extreme end of essentially swallowing their anger for a time.

On the other end of the spectrum, some people with BPD will express their anger explosively, even making verbal threats towards others and sometimes becoming involved in physical fights.

Many people with BPD will flip from one extreme to another.

It is much the same scenario for other emotions as well, especially shame.

There may be suppression of emotion, and masking it from others, or attempts to remain cut off from the experience of emotions, as they are experienced intensely by persons with trauma responses.

On the other hand, there is the surrender of control of emotion as the individual tries to preserve the integrity of his or her own emotional responses. This is the essence of trying to show someone how badly you are hurting by amplifying the emotional response. And as you will find in this workbook, these strong emotions often spill over into the other areas of behaviors and relationships. And while they are not effective, they are still attempts to connect with others, communicate needs and to regulate powerful emotions.

This workbook offers **techniques and strategies** for learning how to better regulate your emotions, including the practice of knowing and labeling your emotional experiences, engaging in behaviors to change your emotions and integrating lifestyle changes to reduce your vulnerability to intense emotions.

With the DBT model, the solution lies not in getting rid of emotions, since emotions are fundamentally adaptive; but rather learning how to reduce the extremes of suppressing or over-expressing emotions and finding ways to land on middle ground between the two extremes.

⊙ The Unstable 5: **Behaviors**

Individuals who have suffered trauma can get caught in cycles of repeating abuse toward themselves or others. Those with BPD frequently engage in several impulsive — and often dangerous — behaviors such as self-harm and suicidal behaviors.

Many people with BPD also exhibit frequent spending, alcohol and eating binges, as well as dangerous sexual encounters.

These are the behaviors that are often the cause of referral for treatment or in-patient hospitalization. And many of these behaviors lead to injured relationships and damaged self-respect, or even a complete loss of sense of self.

The first order of business in this workbook will be for you to learn how to control these behaviors that we will refer to as "target" behaviors since they are **targets for change**.

This is especially true for **high-crisis behaviors such as self-harm and suicidal behaviors**.

This is important as these behaviors will not only be obstacles to your progress with improving in the other areas, but because these behaviors lead to a greater void and suicide tends to appear as more of an option.

The chapter on Crisis Survival will provide you tools with facing crises without making things worse than they are already, and for tolerating painful emotions while cultivating a willingness to stay alive and maneuver skillfully through your emotional pain.

There is also a chapter that helps you assess impulsive behaviors, and then apply specific skills to change those behaviors and maintain your changes using self-management skills.

You may be familiar with the experience of having others accuse you of being manipulative, attention-seeking or needy when you engage in these behaviors.

In this workbook we will emphasize how these behaviors are actually attempts to solve problems. As you already know, the behaviors have caused more problems of their own and **change is essential**.

Each of these behaviors has a function, or a purpose, and they work somewhat, which is why they are maintained and become patterns. The skills in this workbook will help you learn how to ask for help when you need it, and how to manage yourself effectively when you don't get the help you need — without resorting to destructive behaviors.

⊙ The Unstable 5: **Relationships**

Relationships for people with BPD are often emotionally intense, erratic and very stormy. And yet, even in the stormiest of relationships, people with BPD have a hard time letting go of relationships, and, in fact, will often engage in outrageous behaviors in an attempt to prevent the end of these relationships.

These behaviors can result in mixed outcomes. Sometimes they are effective in eliciting help and validation, as well as keeping others close by. In other cases, the other person, bewildered and overwhelmed, ends the relationship, bringing on the opposite result of what the person was wanting. As all people do, persons with BPD do well in healthy and stable relationships, and where they have people who are willing to support them, learn about the disorder and work with it in a manner that supports constructive change, without isolating the person as a problem unto themselves.

Another hallmark of BPD is an all-or-nothing attitude toward people, such as over-idealizing someone. Perhaps you just met someone, but as time goes on and you experience the inevitable let-down that is inherent in relationships that progress for any length of time, you suddenly see that person as completely worthless, evil or unworthy of trust.

This all-or-nothing outlook can change in that moment, and can lead to problems in not guarding your safety or privacy and sets you up for tremendous pain when the person does make a mistake.

This workbook has specific **relationship skills** that will help you change the way you relate with others, including how to ask for what you want and need, how to tolerate "no," and how to build and enhance existing relationships.

You will learn how to say "no," as well as ask for what you want and need, balancing these with your self-respect, so that you can feel better about how you interact with others, which includes accepting others in their human, imperfect state.

We have seen a number of clients overcome their severe behavioral targets and cultivate meaningful and healthier relationships.

⊘ The Unstable 5: **Thought Patterns**

Do you often have very rigid categories of thinking that consists of black or white, all or nothing, or either/or patterns?

These thought patterns are related to emotional states during which angry thoughts arise when anger is triggered. This is very normal in the process of emotions.

However, if you are unaware of what you are thinking, and don't change thoughts, or the direction of your mind, anger can become amplified, thereby making it more intense. Also, if you hold to these rigid thinking categories mentioned above, it could lead to a personal dilemma.

For example, you might make a mistake and consequently feel utter disappointment in yourself and see only the bad in that moment.

Instead, you should consider the mistake along with all the things you do well, **allowing both positive and negative thoughts** of yourself to be present.

Either/or thinking is similar in that either you have to have your act together 100 percent of the time, or you see yourself as a bum who can't hold his or her life together. And if you're feeling bad about yourself or someone else, and the rigid thinking patterns kick in, you will feel worse.

Once again, it is imperative to understand the facts: that it is possible to have good qualities and capabilities and be fallible, all at the same time, and that in a given moment you are not a done product, forever fixed in that bad moment.

One more feature associated with BPD thought patterns — or a problem of cognition — is the problem of dissociation ranging from that daydream state, a bit like a mild trance, to more severe dissociation which seems related to stress and usually clears up once the stress has subsided.

Dissociation can be severe enough that you may feel unreal or outside of your body which can lead to gaps in memory and inhibit learning new skills and effective behaviors. This is essentially a form of "checking out." This particular problem can be countered with skills from the crisis survival chapter and with the skills from mindfulness, helping you to maintain contact with yourself and with reality as it were.

You may also experience dissociation, which may range from a mild trance-like state or a thousand-yard stare to depersonalization, or feeling disconnected from your body.

These symptoms are usually brought on by stress and clear up once the stressor has subsided. Dissociation is common among people who have experienced trauma, and a large number of individuals who suffer with Borderline Personality Disorder have a history of some form of abuse committed against them — often in childhood and sometimes later in life.

For those who have experienced trauma, dissociation acts as a shield against traumas. Over time, dissociative behavior states can be over-generalized and too broadly applied to non-traumatic stressful situations and eventually interfere in work, relationships and in the learning of new behavioral skills and therapeutic progress.

In upcoming chapters you will learn about dialectical thinking which provides a framework and skills for becoming more **flexible of mind**. You will learn to become more familiar with the use of the word and how to observe when your thoughts are polarizing into either/or and other rigid thinking.

Additionally, strategies will be introduced for countering internalized messages of self-invalidation or self-dismissal that are obstacles to cultivating the life that you want.

⊙ The Unstable 5: **Relationship to Self**

Finally, many individuals who have been severely traumatized develop an overwhelming internal emptiness. This sense of emptiness is quite frightening to them, and adds to distress and a sense of dread. Often a sense of self is based on consistent factors in our lives such as study, work, hobbies and relationships that build over years providing us a sense of mastery and an environment that reciprocally provides us feedback that shapes our sense of identity.

Long-term repercussions can occur if there is a history of living in invalidating environments from very early years, in which expressions of emotional experiences — especially the communication of their emotions — were dismissed or met with neglect (a form of invalidation), and/or met with punishment, such as violence.

These experiences may lead you to mistrust your own perceptions and emotional responses, and can lead even to mistrusting your own intuition about potentially harmful situations or people, or to not know what you prefer socially, personally or with respect to educational or vocational pursuits.

Then later, if you have done self-harm or attempted suicide, you have become your own victimizer and the abuse you survived becomes an internal prison. **You become your own enemy. This is new trauma that can seem inescapable**.

When this happens, often individuals look to others for cues about how they should feel, act, or even what they should prefer. This is a very difficult way to live. Not trusting your own intuition and preferences can be quite distressing. Additionally, it is not uncommon then to have a poor self-image and feel chronically bad about yourself.

The chapter on Self will address these issues, providing you with tools and exercises on developing a renewed sense of self. You will define your own preferences and wishes, asserting them even to yourself.

✸ *in* Summary

BPD is a serious disorder that has long-standing consequences for the affected individual and their loved ones. The experience is one of misery, suffering, and in some cases, loss of personal identity.

Having emphasized the importance of professional assessment for the purposes of formal diagnosis, the following chapter will provide simple self-evaluative tools that may be helpful to persons who have yet to seek professional assessment, and will be helpful in building awareness and in understanding the symptoms associated with BPD. Hopefully, this workbook will assist you in making progress in understanding yourself in a more compassionate light and empowering you to make progress in your **pursuit of wellness**.

Chapter II

WHAT IS DIALECTICAL BEHAVIOR THERAPY?

DBT, as a treatment model, falls under the large psychotherapy umbrella of cognitive behavioral therapy. DBT targets areas of thought patterns, such as dysregulation of thought, and behavioral patterns such as the behaviors outlined in Chapter One.

✿ DBT: **Behavioral Skills**

DBT has a very heavy behavioral emphasis. In other words, from the start, action must be taken to **identify and change behaviors**, especially those life-threatening in nature, and behaviors that threaten the life of the therapeutic relationship.

Many people with BPD are often referred to a DBT practitioner following one or more episodes of self-harm, suicide attempts or threats to commit suicide.

And since there is a logical necessity for a client to continue living in order to benefit from the treatment, DBT's number one mission is equipping people with survival skills so that they can live to see how well DBT can work for them. This is a critical skill because the intense and strenuous nature of suicidal and self-harm behaviors often can, and does, threaten the life of the therapeutic relationship.

In this book, you will learn more about behavioral and learning principles and relapse prevention, and you will find the principles peppered throughout. As you will find later, DBT especially targets impulsive and reactive behaviors that are typically mood-dependent, helping you to construct the **healthy and fulfilling life** you want.

DBT provides an array of behaviors, or actions, that a person with BPD can implement right away with concrete activities, or skills, as we will be referring to them.

In your case, you will be reading about these principles and applying them the best you can. In doing so, you will learn to monitor and assess your actions in great detail in order that you may glean what works and what doesn't work for you to overcome these behaviors, and what **strengthens your motivation** to continue in your practice — even when you feel discouraged.

✿ DBT: **Emotional Skills**

We've already stated that the core problem with BPD, according to the DBT model, is that of emotion dysregulation. Emotion dysregulation arises from a combination of our highly sensitive emotional system rooted in biology and a history of chronic invalidation that leaves you unequipped to skillfully manage your emotional experiences.

DBT offers a framework for **understanding emotions** as well as multiple skills for increasing awareness of your emotions as you experience them, tolerating your strong emotional states, countering strong emotions and impulses, as well as learning how to do the opposite of what your mood or your emotions are telling you to do.

DBT: Non-Judgmental Skills

You will be learning a new set of thinking skills to **overcome old habits of thought**, including overly rigid categories of thought about yourself, others and the world at large.

You will learn skills to challenge and change any habits of thought such as self-invalidating statements. **Mindfulness skills** in DBT also assist you with not only building awareness regarding what you're thinking, but increasing your control over where those thoughts go, increasing your mind control as it were, even countering dissociation.

DBT: Relationship Skills

DBT provides three broad categories of interpersonal skills including:

1) how to ask for something you want or how to say "**no**"
2.) how to maintain a good relationship
3) how to maintain your self-respect as you deal with others

You will learn to integrate all of these skills together and keep them in balance. Often conflicts with others arise from assumptions that are untested and often incorrect.

DBT: Developing a Sense of Self

The chapter related to targets of self will include awareness-building exercises challenging you to envision about the **kind of life you want**. Not just in a fantastical kind of way, but in a real world way — translating visions into planning and engaging in activities that you enjoy. Knowing and stating your preferences and engaging in consistent behaviors that, over time, increase a sense of mastery, quality and joy.

Chapter III

DBT: THE KEY CONCEPTS

While DBT falls within the psychotherapeutic realm of cognitive behavioral therapy in that it directly addresses behavior change and control, and directly targets thinking patterns and their role in a person's psychological health, it differs greatly from standard cognitive behavioral therapies in a few ways. The emphasis on both acceptance and change, as well as dialectics, define those differences:

1. Acceptance & Change

2. Dialectics

3. Behavioral Principles

unpacking the principles
Acceptance & Change

DBT emphasizes **acceptance**, which takes where you are at this moment in time and says: "given your history and current level of skillfulness, you are doing the very best that you can." Even if you are currently facing chaotic relationships or self-respect damaging behaviors, no matter how much you or your therapist wish things were otherwise, they are not. And to not accept these as facts is refusing to acknowledge reality. DBT challenges you to practice **accepting yourself** and your situation, just as it is.

Acceptance is *not* the same as approval. It's not saying, "Gee, my life is unbearable. That's great." Through acceptance you can begin to see some of the *why* regarding your current responses to your situation: "Given biological factors, my past experiences and my current skills, I'm doing the best that I can."

Acceptance is **letting go** of useless judgments that only complicate your life and do nothing to make things better for you. It is simply and plainly acknowledging the facts as they are.

In balance to acceptance, DBT also promotes change. Although you are indeed doing the very best that you can at this time, you also need to **change your behaviors**.

Furthermore, not only do you need to change your behaviors, you must try harder and do better in order to incorporate new skills in your life. You need to change your emotional experiences, your impulsive behaviors, and your relationships by doing better and trying harder. These changes will not come by magic or coincidence, but only through your **willingness** and your **hard work**.

By mentioning this emphasis on both acceptance and change we are already moving into the idea of **dialectics**.

In this section, we will discuss why your progress does not depend on either acceptance or change, but through *both* acceptance and change. And you may find it difficult, as do DBT clients and therapists, to find a balance between these polar opposites. And you will find that from time to time, you will slide into emphasizing one over the other. And that's ok. The bottom line is, you are moving in the right direction.

Dialectics

Inspirational writer Parker Palmer wrote about his spiritual life in these terms: "Contradiction, paradox, the tension of opposites: these have always been at the heart of my experience, and I think I'm not alone. I'm tugged one way and then the other. My beliefs and actions often seem at odds. My strengths are sometimes cancelled by my weaknesses. My self, and the world around me, seem more a study in dissonance than a harmony of the integrated whole."

His words illustrate well the inherence of opposites, or polarities, and that life is riddled with inescapable tugging, pushing and pulling in many directions.

This experience of feeling scattered or stretched is very much a common experience, and one that is certainly felt by people who suffer with Borderline Personality Disorder.

To those with the disorder, it is the attempt to live in the impossibility of polarized categories of either/or (also frequently insisted upon by those around them) that aggravates their lives as they strive for these unattainable ends.

Acknowledging these tensions as inherent and present allows individuals to consider **new patterns of living** that suggests there is a kernel of truth on each end of the pole, and makes it possible to loosen the tight grip of either/or living.

So dialectics is a framework for acknowledging contradictory urges, thoughts and actions that are inherent in life and bring with them a certain tension. It's a way of thinking in identifying contradictions and polar opposites in life and seeks to find what lies between the two poles, or what lies between extremes of emotion, thought and relationships, acknowledging the truth in everything around us.

Moving into a dialectical mode, you can validate the importance for emotional control to lead an effective life. We all need that.

People with good emotional control tend to do better in school and work and relationships. There may be something in your life that is a cause for great sadness, but you still have to function at work and school. It's probably not acceptable to your managers to express your sorrow to your customers since that's not your function. Or if you're at school, say college, your professors aren't likely to indulge your expression of emotions in class.

You can control your emotions without simply dismissing them or trying to pretend that you're a non-emotional being. Continuing in the dialectical mode, you can also validate and accept you feel what you feel, and even express that to other people.

Of course, since you may be well-versed in the either/or mode, and you may have a biological vulnerability to powerful emotions, this all sounds very risky.

But as you learn the skills in this book you will feel equipped with new tools to **change your emotional experiences** so that you can both more effectively control emotions and express emotions without necessarily melting down.

What we are talking about here is identifying the validity of both emotional control and expression, moving these poles closer to one another through practice, eventually finding a synthesis between the two.

While control and expression are opposed to another dialectically, creating tension that can be painful, over-control and the meltdown are representative of polarization, which should be avoided.

Wholeness

The dialectics emphasize wholeness, looking at how parts fit into the whole of a system, how pieces of a puzzle fit together in a relationship to form a complete picture. Following a "bad" behavior or an episode of "acting out," you resolve to never repeat your mistakes, and this oversimplification of problem-solving leaves you without practical skills to change, thus leaving you to likely repeat the behavior and again endure the judgments of others and yourself for failing. You and people who know you think you're the problem: all the pain surrounding your impulsive behaviors and your bad moods are the result of your poor thinking. It's all your fault.

Therefore if there is no family support, no steady employment and there is drug addiction and poverty that has ruled for generations, and if violence is a regular part of upbringing as a way to solve differences, then we begin to see a more whole and more clear picture of the motivations for behaviors, as well the functions of the behaviors. You have to take these steps to find wholeness. It is not all your fault, but it is up to you to solve your problems.

Behavioral Principles

As a behavioral therapy, DBT places tremendous importance on principles of learning and reinforcement. It considers behaviors, both effective and ineffective, as under the influence of reinforcers, and reinforces or strengthens the likelihood that you will repeat a given behavior.

As you journey through this workbook, you will learn how to identify the reinforcers, also called consequences, of your behaviors. As you learn about reinforcers, and begin to identify them in relationship to your behaviors, you will discover how your behaviors are learned and then maintained by the reinforcers specific to you.

Those who suffer with Borderline Personality Disorder are often frustrated with the fact that they repeatedly engage in impulsive behaviors they actually desire to not do, usually attributing their repeated failures to traits that we mentioned above (moral weakness, selfishness, etc.).

For the purpose of illustrating this principle of reinforcement, let's consider a smoking habit.

Many people who smoke have factual data that leads them to understand that smoking is harmful to their health, especially if they do it with great frequency and chronically.

However, this information is not enough for them to quit smoking. Why do people keep smoking when they know for a fact that smoking is bad for them?

Let's look at the common reinforcers for smoking, that is, the **function within the dysfunction**. For one, chemically, smoking breaks the blood-brain barrier instantly, affecting areas of the brain. The nicotine gets to the brain ASAP!

This is one reason it's a difficult habit to break. And to avoid the agitation of withdrawal a smoker smokes again, giving smoking a function, making it effective to avoid agitation in the short run, despite the long-term health risks.

Other secondary reinforcers may include things such as "smokers bond" that can occur. Friendship and bonding happen around the act of smoking. Come rain or shine, hard-core smokers will meet, huddled together outside. This sense of affiliation develops, because only smokers know the hardship of smoking in an increasingly anti-smoking world.

There is a shared experience, a sense of fun, perhaps even a sense of being among rebels. All of these factors and others are what strengthen a person's propensity to engage in smoking behavior, even if they are determined to quit.

Many behaviors, that in the long run are harmful to you, have immediate reinforcers that follow the behavior. People who overeat when they are sad sometimes feel less sad or distracted from their emotional pain. Perhaps they even have a sense of control in a life that they feel they have very little control in. More severe behaviors also have these "hidden" functions of bringing a sense of calm, focus and control to otherwise miserable conditions of emotional suffering.

Within the DBT framework, dysfunctional behaviors are considered attempts at problem-solving, rather than just pure "craziness." And when dysfunctional behaviors work well enough, while being reinforced, they are likely to stick around.

In this workbook, behaviors are analyzed with an eye for finding out what it is that is reinforcing a behavior, what it is about a given behavior that *works*, at least in the short term.

There is also an eye out for what it will take to **reinforce new behaviors** and weaken reinforcers for behaviors that you wish to stop doing.

As you move through this workbook, you will discover the reinforcers that encourage the behaviors that you are trying to change. You will also discover the importance of reinforcement for increasing your new **skillful responses to situations**.

You see, many people make the mistake of thinking they can guilt themselves into new positive behaviors. That is, they try to punish themselves into the desired behaviors such as emotional control or assertiveness.

This is that oversimplified trait-based approach once again rearing its ugly head. The problem here is that these measures are punitive and have no effect for producing new behaviors.

If you take the punitive approach, which you may have already tried at least a thousand times, you will only demoralize yourself without changing behaviors.

As you will come to see, the best way to increase new effective behaviors, will be to introduce **reinforcers for your new behaviors** so that they are more likely to stick, and eventually become truly learned.

We will later especially focus on **positive reinforcement**, and you will also use exercises in this book to learn how to practice monitoring and defining behaviors, how to establish plans of action for change, and how to recover from setbacks.

✱ *in* Summary

In this chapter, we discussed DBT as a cognitive behavioral treatment for BPD. It is a structured therapy that prioritizes treatment targets and emphasizes **acceptance balanced with change**. The framework of dialectics addresses symptoms of borderline personality disorder as the result and the function of biological vulnerabilities within an invalidating environment that is dismissive of basic expression of negative emotions and bids for connection, while attending to and reinforcing displays of emotional escalation and crisis behaviors, thus contributing to the development of the emotional and psychological issues addressed in this book

Chapter IV

SELF-ASSESSMENT TOOLS FOR BPD

According to DBT, the defining feature of BPD is emotional dysregulation, and according to the DBT biosocial model, BPD is a function of emotional vulnerability coupled with an invalidating environment.

Assessing Yourself

As you will come to learn in this workbook, many of the crisis-centered behaviors commonly associated with BPD are, to a great degree, effective at reducing intense emotional turmoil momentarily. However, the maladaptive coping mechanisms will increase the emotional turmoil exponentially over time.

In this section of the workbook you will complete 5 questionnaires to assess your current level of emotional dysregulation. These self-assessments will assist in awareness-building about your general experiences which in turn will assist you in assessing effective courses of action for regulating your emotional states with the skills that you will learn in this workbook.

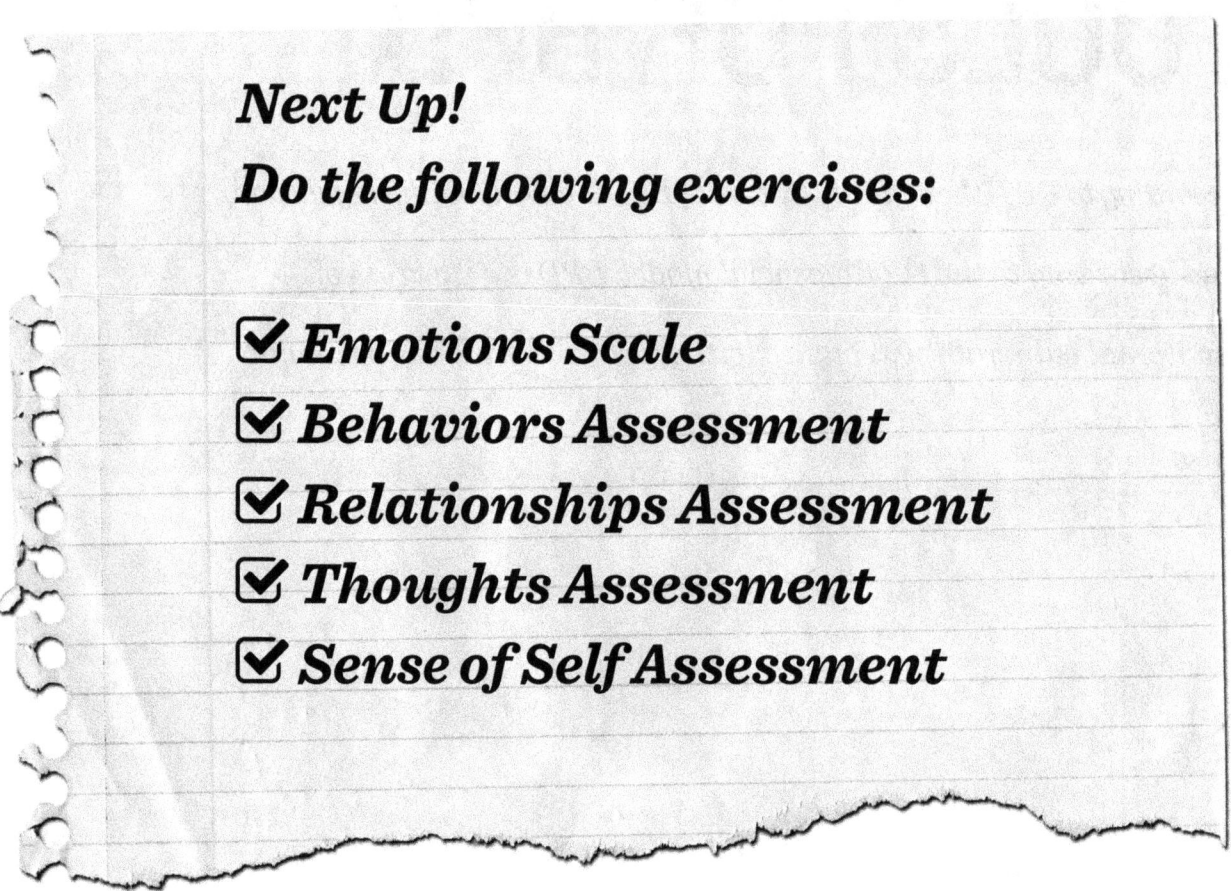

Next Up!
Do the following exercises:

- ☑ *Emotions Scale*
- ☑ *Behaviors Assessment*
- ☑ *Relationships Assessment*
- ☑ *Thoughts Assessment*
- ☑ *Sense of Self Assessment*

 **Exercise:**

ASSESSING YOUR EMOTIONS

Using the following checklist, place a check mark in each box next to each statement that you believe reflects your experience of your emotions. For each statement that you check, use the rating scale to indicate your overall experience of what is described in the statement, or how powerfully it resonates with you.

The scale provided is a simple 0 to 5
0 = not at all
1 = minimal
2 = mild
3 = moderate
4 = strong
5 = intense

Emotional Experience Checklist. Rate (0 to 5):

☐ *I generally feel irritable.*
○ ○ ○ ○ ○

☐ *I frequently feel anxious.*
○ ○ ○ ○ ○

☐ *On more days than not, I feel like hiding.*
○ ○ ○ ○ ○

☐ *I'm emotionally reactive.*
○ ○ ○ ○ ○

☐ *I hate my emotions.*
○ ○ ○ ○ ○

☐ *I'm usually emotionally intense.*
○ ○ ○ ○ ○

☐ *I frequently become enraged.*
○ ○ ○ ○ ○

☐ *I often try to hide, suppress or blunt my emotions.*
○ ○ ○ ○ ○

☐ *It doesn't take much to set me off.*
○ ○ ○ ○ ○

☐ *I often feel ashamed of myself.*
○ ○ ○ ○ ○

☐ *I have little or no control over my emotions.*

○ ○ ○ ○ ○

☐ *I tend to worry a lot.*
○ ○ ○ ○ ○

☐ *My emotions are all over the place.*
○ ○ ○ ○ ○

☐ *I'm rarely happy or in a good mood.*
○ ○ ○ ○ ○

Total number of checked statements: _____

If you checked seven or more of these items with an intensity of 3 or greater, this indicates that you likely have trouble regulating your emotions, and this may be saying what you already know. Problems with regulating your emotions will be addressed in subsequent chapters on emotion regulation, including skills practices for reducing your vulnerability to negative emotions.

✏️ Exercise:
ASSESSING YOUR BEHAVIORS

Follow the same guidelines as with the previous assessment. Please bear in mind that these questions touch on some sensitive behaviors that are common among individuals who struggle with BPD. This assessment may be best completed when you are feeling your best, and are not feeling especially vulnerable. Or if you are working with a therapist, this may be an exercise you suggest be completed during one of your sessions.

The scale provided is a simple 0 to 5
0 = not at all
1 = minimal
2 = mild
3 = moderate
4 = strong
5 = intense

Assessing Your Behaviors Checklist. Rate (0 to 5):

☐ *I do impulsive things that I'm ashamed of.*
○ ○ ○ ○ ○

☐ *Sometimes I eat until I feel like bursting.*
○ ○ ○ ○ ○

☐ *I shop to make myself feel better.*
○ ○ ○ ○ ○

☐ *I frequently can't control my behaviors.*
○ ○ ○ ○ ○

☐ *Others have commented on my "crazy" behaviors.*
○ ○ ○ ○ ○

☐ *I have deliberately injured myself.*
○ ○ ○ ○ ○

☐ *Sometimes I have five alcoholic beverages or more in one setting.*
○ ○ ○ ○ ○

☐ *I have at least once threatened to others to kill myself.*
○ ○ ○ ○ ○

☐ *I frequently drive recklessly, or under the influence of substances.*
○ ○ ○ ○ ○

☐ *I engaged in high-risk sexual behavior in the last year.*
○ ○ ○ ○ ○

☐ *I have attempted to overdose at least once.*
○ ○ ○ ○ ○

☐ *I frequently abuse my prescription medications.*
○ ○ ○ ○ ○

☐ *I have attempted at least once to end my own life.*
○ ○ ○ ○ ○

☐ *I have on several occasions been in physical fights.*
○ ○ ○ ○ ○

☐ *I rely on drugs or alcohol to feel normal or better.*
○ ○ ○ ○ ○

If you checked seven or more of these statements with an intensity of 3 or greater, this may indicate that you have trouble **regulating your behaviors** in a manner that is not mood-dependent and that is counterproductive to leading an effective lifestyle in order to move closer to your goals for a better life. Chapters on Crisis Survival Skills and Self Management will help you address these problems. These skills will focus on how to bear your emotional pain in a skillful manner without making crises worse, and the self-management procedures will assist you in analyzing your behaviors so that you can develop specific plans for changing them.

✏️ Exercise:
ASSESSING YOUR RELATIONSHIPS

Using the same method above, check the boxes below that you believe are representative of your relationships.

The scale provided is a simple 0 to 5
0 = not at all
1 = minimal
2 = mild
3 = moderate
4 = strong
5 = intense

Assessing Your Relationships Checklist. Rate (0 to 5):

☐ *I don't believe that I'm lovable.*
○ ○ ○ ○ ○

☐ *No one understands me or the things I've been through.*
○ ○ ○ ○ ○

☐ *Many of my relationships start great, and then quickly go to hell.*
○ ○ ○ ○ ○

☐ *I can become intimate, or want to, very early on in relationships.*
○ ○ ○ ○ ○

☐ *I try to be a good person to win the approval of others.*
○ ○ ○ ○ ○

☐ *When others can't spend time with me, it's because they hate me.*
○ ○ ○ ○ ○

☐ *In dating relationships, I fall in love very quickly.*
○ ○ ○ ○ ○

☐ *I end relationships where I think the other person will dump me.*
○ ○ ○ ○ ○

☐ *It's very difficult for me to make new friends.*
○○○○○

☐ *I can totally love someone one minute, and hate them the next.*
○○○○○

☐ *I often disappoint others and am frequently misunderstood.*
○○○○○

☐ *I have been told I'm smothering or obsessive in relationships.*
○○○○○

☐ *My relationships are usually very intense and rocky.*
○○○○○

☐ *Friends and relatives seem afraid of me and avoid being around me.*
○○○○○

☐ *Other people don't take me seriously and are disrespectful.*
○○○○○

If you checked seven or more of these statements with an intensity of 3 or greater, then it is likely that you have trouble **regulating relationships**, whether they are with friends, relatives or love interests. It's not all you, as you will come to find as you work your way through the chapter on skills for relationships. You will learn strategies for creating new relationships, as well as skills for enhancing existing relationships. You will also develop skills and strategies to meet personal objectives and increase your self-respect, whether in the workplace, school, with friends or in your family.

✏️ Exercise:
ASSESSING YOUR THOUGHTS

Again, use the same check and rate procedure as you have with the previous assessments, checking those statements that you believe are representative of your typical or usual patterns and style of thinking about yourself, others and the world you live in.

The scale provided is a simple 0 to 5
0 = not at all
1 = minimal
2 = mild
3 = moderate
4 = strong
5 = intense

☐ *I think that most people are either good or bad.*
○ ○ ○ ○ ○

☐ *I believe I'm incapable of solving my problems.*
○ ○ ○ ○ ○

☐ *I frequently "zone out" or feel like I've left my body.*
○ ○ ○ ○ ○

☐ *I usually think of myself in very negative terms.*
○ ○ ○ ○ ○

☐ *I can have a one-track mind when it comes to disagreements.*
○ ○ ○ ○ ○

☐ *I see the world in terms of black or white and right or wrong.*
○ ○ ○ ○ ○

☐ *When I'm stressed, I want to be alone to be able to think.*
○ ○ ○ ○ ○

☐ *I have at least once threatened to others to kill myself.*
○ ○ ○ ○ ○

☐ *I sometimes think coworkers or relatives are out to get me.*
○○○○○

☐ *I sometimes have intrusive thoughts of self-harm.*
○○○○○

☐ *Sometimes I can't remember something that was just said to me, but others things I remember in great detail.*
○○○○○

☐ *I often think about dying.*
○○○○○

☐ *I fired the last therapist that was late to an appointment.*
○○○○○

☐ *I believe people should always treat me decently.*
○○○○○

☐ *People who don't give me what I want are jerks, or evil.*
○○○○○

☐ *I can't help but think about how hopeless I am.*
○○○○○

If you checked seven or more of these statements with an intensity of 3 or greater this may indicate you have trouble **regulating your thoughts**. In some cases, this may be due to dissociative or paranoid responses to stress, and/or due to rigid and polarized (as opposed to finding synthesis) thinking that lacks flexibility. **Thought regulation skills** will come later to help you develop a resistance to dissociation and to increase flexibility in how you think of yourself, others and the world, with the practice of acceptance and dialectical thinking.

✏️ Exercise:
ASSESSING YOUR SENSE OF SELF

This is the final self-assessment for this chapter. Once again, check and rate the statements that you believe are representative of your typical experience for yourself.

The scale provided is a simple 0 to 5
0 = not at all
1 = minimal
2 = mild
3 = moderate
4 = strong
5 = intense

☐ *I usually disregard my own preferences in order to please other people.*
○ ○ ○ ○ ○

☐ *I tend to jump from job to job and from one interest to another.*
○ ○ ○ ○ ○

☐ *I feel empty inside, or like there is a hole inside of me.*
○ ○ ○ ○ ○

☐ *I tend to copy or emulate the style of other people.*
○ ○ ○ ○ ○

☐ *I need other people to tell me how I'm doing in most areas of life.*
○ ○ ○ ○ ○

☐ *I try to be or do what other people want me to be or do.*
○ ○ ○ ○ ○

☐ *I often feel disconnected from the world.*
○ ○ ○ ○ ○

☐ *I rarely know what I want from myself or others.*
○ ○ ○ ○ ○

☐ *I often feel numb or don't feel anything.*
○○○○○

☐ *I'm easily influenced by the opinions of others.*
○○○○○

☐ *After completing activities or driving, I don't recall doing it.*
○○○○○

☐ *I frequently feel like I'm in a dreamy fog.*
○○○○○

☐ *Even as an adult, I don't know what I want to do with my life.*
○○○○○

☐ *I have on several occasions been in physical fights.*
○○○○○

☐ *I don't have a consistent dress style, education or work experience.*
○○○○○

If you checked seven or more of these statements with an intensity of 3 or greater, this may indicate that you have trouble with **regulation of self**, and may even feel as though you lack an identity, or lack consistency in important areas of life leaving you without something that is identifiably yours such as an interest, hobby, skill or vocation.

Later on you will work through skills that address developing your preferences, tastes and basic mastery, and these skills can become tools that assist you in developing consistency so that you will more likely come to know who you are and develop a **stronger sense of self**, including strategies for countering dissociative symptoms.

✱ *in* Summary

As with the completion of any assessment come the next steps. We will begin to move into learning more about specific areas of your life to **target for change**. In upcoming chapters, we will provide further information on these specific areas:

1. **Emotions**
2. **Behaviors**
3. **Thoughts**
4. **Relationships**
5. **Sense of Self**

Each chapter will provide you with more detailed information about problems in these areas common to those who suffer with BPD, and each chapter will contain assessments and exercises to help you continue building your awareness of these problems, and to begin to engage you in practices to help you change.

THE IMPORTANCE OF PROFESSIONAL ASSESSMENT

We cannot stress enough the importance of professional assessment by a mental health professional qualified to assess you before proceeding with formal diagnosis. Diagnosis should inform the progression into and the mode of treatment that follows. It's not enough to read a book, or an informational website to self-diagnose, just in the same way you wouldn't want to count on self-diagnoses for medical conditions such as cancer, diabetes or asthma.

You need to see a licensed clinician. Statutes, laws and ethics that have been developed to protect the public vary from one state to another, and will determine who is qualified to assess you and to make or rule out a diagnosis, as will factors related to education and training.

Mental health professionals you are likely to seek out or encounter in professional practice may include psychiatrists, psychologists, professional counselors, clinical social workers, or marriage and family therapists.

In closing this chapter, let us say that a major factor in your success in working with a therapist will be greatly influenced by your **commitment to the therapy**, your attendance at scheduled sessions, and your **practice of skills** and homework assigned by your therapist.

For success, you need to commit to working with a therapist and learning DBT skills for a minimum of **one year**. If any difficulties arise in your relationship with your therapist, make sure you address those rather than quitting.

Chapter V

GETTING TO WISE MIND

*Mindfulness is the **core skill** in DBT. You might think of it as a center of a bicycle wheel, with the other skills being the spokes all converging and intersecting there at the center. You will need mindfulness to become increasingly effective with the other skills. When you practice crisis survival skills, emotion regulation, or relationship skills, the more mindful you are, the more effective you will be.*

LIVING IN YOUR LIFE: WHAT IS MINDFULNESS?

Mindfulness, which can be described in a thousand ways, is at the very least a practice in paying attention. It's about **expanding your awareness** to your experiences, your emotions, your behaviors, and your thoughts. This includes the world around you, the things you long for, and the things you fear.

Mindfulness also may be described as seeing, truly seeing, with clarity; seeing things as they are without necessarily trying to change them. As you begin your practice of mindfulness you may see more vividly the clutter of your mind's racing thoughts, self-condemnation and impulsive behaviors.

You may also see more clearly your own vision for what you want your life to look like: free of emotional suffering, connected in **secure relationships**, and free from the tyranny of impulsivity.

Mindfulness is about living in or with yourself, even becoming more genuinely interested in yourself and your own life. We might even say mindfulness helps you to be **at home with yourself**. Mindfulness practice addresses problems with dissociation, or that experience of zoning out.

You don't have to check out when you face stressful situations even though that may be a pattern for you at this moment. We simply have to accept that. If that's the case, then that's the case. But since dissociation creates problems in memory, learning, and effective engagement with your life, it must change. Mindfulness also helps you to develop increased tolerance for your strong emotions.

Mindfulness won't make your emotions less strong, but your practice will move you closer to allowing your primary emotional responses to be what they truly are: normal and fundamentally adaptive.

As you practice simply noticing your emotional responses without complicating them with judgments or non-acceptance, you will perhaps begin to see them anew as friends that provide you with motivation, and with information about things going on around you, as well as assist you in connecting in relationships.

Your practice of these **mindfulness skills untangle complicated thoughts**: the judgments, the self-invalidation, and the exaggerations of either/or thinking as you discover that many of the "shoulds" you have come to believe in are conditioned assumptions that don't always square with the facts.

If you let yourself, you will come to tune out many misconceptions about yourself: "I shouldn't be so sensitive," "I should just suck it up," "I should always have it all together." In your practice of mindfulness, you will just notice these thoughts, simply see them without acting on them, and perhaps with some regularity challenge them with questions such as "Well, why shouldn't I be so sensitive?" "Why should I just suck it up?" and "Why should I have it all together, and what does that mean anyway?"

Applied to your behaviors, mindfulness will help you see more clearly situations where you are more vulnerable to impulsivity, and the experience of impulse urges rising up inside of you when you become agitated, frightened or lonely.

Just recognizing these urges without reacting to them can provide you with some space to choose alternate courses of actions, perhaps turning toward exercise, music, reading, prayer and other activities instead. Just noticing your self-destructive behaviors, factually and without judgment, allows you to see patterns of triggers, behaviors and their consequences, and you can better evaluate them as effective or ineffective. This will result in better information about how to effectively change them with **specific behavioral plans**, rather than getting bogged down in judgments about them.

MINDFULNESS AS MIND CONTROL

Mindfulness in relationships can lead you to fuller enjoyment of loved ones and friends, as you bring your full self, with all of your attention, to a delicious meal, discussion over tea, or play with a child. Having presence in these moments, without becoming distracted by worry or thoughts like "When will the storm return?" "I don't deserve this," or "I'm still miserable" can make it possible for you to just drink in the experience of fun, happiness or joy.

Mindfulness in relationships will help you increase your tolerance for the foibles and fallibility of other people. You can simply notice that your friend is 10 minutes late without assuming that they're blowing you off; you can simply notice the fear of rejection come and go, without reacting to it; you can accept the apologies of others when they have let you down. Mindfulness in relationships will help you to effectively express how you feel toward others, whether through an expression of love, or an expression of disappointment.

LIVING AT HOME WITH YOURSELF: PRACTICING MINDFULNESS

To live at home with yourself, to relinquish rigid demands on yourself and others, to change your focus from fear and self-loathing, you will have to practice. You will have to practice simply noticing your emotions, thoughts and behaviors without reacting to them, or without, as some mindfulness teachers say, attaching to them. You begin by simply noticing these things, just seeing them, and watching them, without applying either/or judgments.

MINDFULNESS IS BOTH SIMPLE AND DIFFICULT

It is simple when you consider that you carry with you at all times the necessary equipment for the practice. That is, you have yourself, and we will explain this a bit more in a moment.

On the other hand, mindfulness is difficult to practice because of the well-conditioned patterns of thought you hold. For all your life, you have likely been taught to think in categories of either/or, and to "should" about everything.

If you hold a fundamental belief that you should be able to solve all of your problems on your own, and you find that you can't do it, you feel terrible for violating the "should."

If you believe other people should always, in every situation, give you what you want, and they don't, you feel terrible about them for not doing what they should. If you believe you should just ignore your negative emotions, but you can't because you experience them regardless of your beliefs, you will think of yourself as a failure, which in turn may trigger a downward spiral into feeling even worse.

Mindfulness is also difficult to practice when you consider our go-go-go world. There is so much noise and clutter, entertainment and enticements to get more, be beautiful, drive this car, that stuff and things are the key to happiness, and so on. We have many conveniences that encourage us to do more in a single instant than what is hardly possible.

Given these factors, it's no wonder that the practice of mindfulness, as we have described it so far, and the exercise you are about to read about and practice, can seem strange, or sound so impossible. Reactive thinking, the to and fro of anxiety, want, and the demands of our multi-task world keep us from awareness. Often the thoughts are contradictory or confused; we vacillate between extremes.

Mindfulness is a practice to bring your attention under your control, to **soothe the mind** and to simplify the activity of your thoughts.

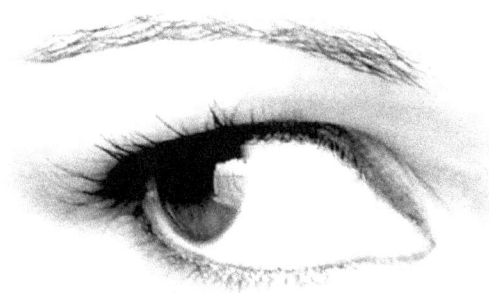 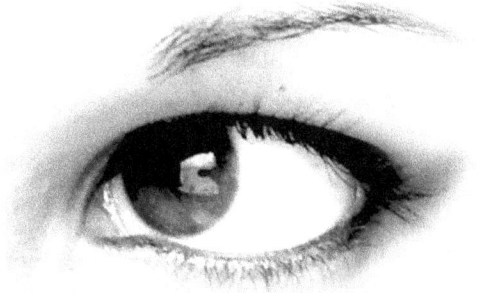

MINDFULNESS BASICS

The following principles are the basics that will guide and shape your practice of mindfulness.

Breathe

Breathing is fundamental to the practice of mindfulness. In every tradition of mindfulness, whatever its root, breathing is key to becoming centered, calm and attentive.

What do we mean by breathe?

We mean changing the path of breath from your normal breathing, which is likely shallow and primarily in the upper portion of your lungs, to the more natural path through the diaphragm and through the lower portion of your lungs for more breath, deeper breath. Singers, well-trained public speakers, actors and practitioners of the martial arts, yoga and meditation all know the power of breathing from the diaphragm.

Notice

We have already covered noticing, or seeing. With respect to your practice of mindfulness, we ask you to practice, through these exercises, noticing what you feel, noticing what you think, noticing what you do, and what you want to do, or what urges you feel toward action. This noticing will become a practice in knowing what you feel, think, do and want to do.

Describe

At this step of your practice, we ask you to describe what you notice in factual terms rather than with judgmental labels.

For example, when you notice that you feel angry, practice saying to yourself, "I feel anger." You can see the simplicity in that, and you may already see the complexity, too, being that at first you will want to let fly with judgments about why you're feeling angry, perhaps wanting to say instead, "My boss is such a jerk, he never treats me fairly, I should quit my job. He makes me so mad." Judgments are so well-conditioned, so it will be a difficult practice, but not impossible.

Engage With Presence

Your practice of mindfulness is not about sitting cross-legged in a dark room repeating mantras, or fantasizing about a life you can't have. Although, be aware that there are some exercises for learning and increasing your skills that require you to withdraw from your normal activities to practice and to recollect yourself when your thoughts and emotions and energies are scattered about.

This practice of mindfulness will also help you cultivate the life you want by **participating in your life**, in each moment as it comes, facing each situation as it is as skillfully as you can at that moment.

Rather than avoiding situations through dissociation, evading conversations that are painful or changing behavioral patterns, you will instead approach them with new tools, and find that you can develop increasing tolerance for difficult tasks, situations and even your own painful emotions. This also requires that you are present for your life, even in difficult situations.

One Thing

Part of your practice will be to engage in one thing at a time, rather than trying to engage in everything at once, which is difficult, and too often overwhelming.

You will practice simplifying how you approach your relationships, behaviors and other tasks, making things easier on yourself.

This element of mindfulness is the practice of selecting what you pay attention to in a given moment, or how you will focus. To stay focused, or concentrated, will require that you choose what activity, situation, thoughts or emotions you focus on,

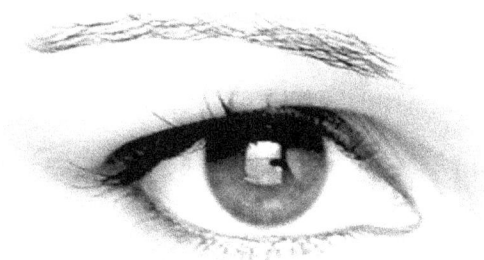
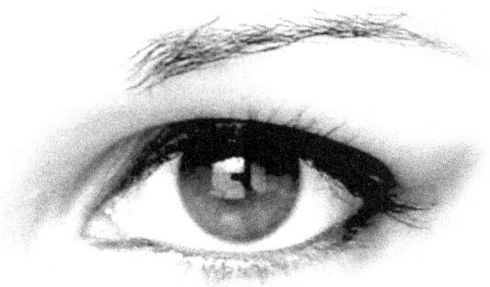

and in turn you can become more selective and deliberate about what you choose to do, and where your mind goes.

The more you slow down, the more **deliberate and focused** you'll be. You'll get more done because you will be able to prioritize tasks, and do them more efficiently and with less mistakes.

✏ Exercise One:
MINDFULNESS EXERCISES

Read the description of each exercise and then practice. Remember, you're not in a contest, no one is keeping track of whether or not you do this right; this is just practice. Each time you practice one of these exercises you will become a little more proficient at it. If you begin your practice and find your mind goes all over the place or leaves your practice, just notice that you're off course, and that your mind has wandered. And then gently bring your mind back to the practice. In fact, you can count on your mind wandering as you begin these exercises ... and bringing your mind back to the practice, over and over and over again is also part of the practice and part of training your mind, as you incrementally gain more awareness and focus.

AWARENESS AND ATTENTION TO YOUR BREATH

We begin with a fairly simple practice. Set aside five minutes. In this exercise you will want to find a relatively quiet place to sit alone in a chair. After seating yourself comfortably, situate yourself so that your body is fairly upright so that you will be able to breathe freely.

You are going to practice breathing, and giving your full attention to your breathing.

Close your eyes so that nothing visually distracts you. Breathe from your belly, from your diaphragm, gently drawing in your breath through your nose and slowly and gently exhaling your breath through your mouth.

Practice this exercise doing the following:

Breathe: From your belly, gently draw in breath through your nose, and gently let the breath out. Don't force it in or out, or try to over-control your breathing. Just let your breath come in and let your breath go out. Repeat this for at least three cycles, allowing you time to settle.

Notice: As you continue breathing, just notice your breath as it enters your nostrils, and as it leaves through your mouth. Notice how it feels entering and exiting gently. Be aware of your breath, giving it your full attention, thinking of nothing else.

Describe: As you continue breathing, describe your experience of breathing. Say to yourself something like: "I feel my chest expanding and falling," or "My breath is soft," or "I feel my breath leaving my mouth." Let go of judgmental thoughts if they come. Don't entertain thoughts about how strange this is, or that it's weird or a waste of time. Let go of thoughts of any other activities that you can get to later. When distracting thoughts come, simply describe them: "I notice a thought about laundry just entered my mind," or "This is difficult." Let go of them and come back to your breath.

Engage with Presence: Stay engaged in this practice. Try to give your full attention to your breath — and only your breath — as it comes in and as it leaves.

Acknowledge that it's difficult, if it is, and stay with it for a few minutes. Stay present with your breathing, giving it your full attention. If you have the urge to quit or to let your mind stray to something you're worried about, turn your focus back toward this moment and your breath, staying with it for just a few minutes.

As much as you are able, don't leave this moment, don't check out, leave mentally or daydream, and don't let your mind wander to thoughts about other places you'd rather be, or things you'd rather be doing. Just stay in this one moment.

One Thing: This is the only thing you are doing when you practice. You are only breathing. And that is all. You're not thinking about anything else, your full attention is on your breath. Again, let go of distracting thoughts or urges. At this moment, this is all that you are doing. You are training your mind to go where you want it to go, you are increasing your focus, and other activities can wait and will be there waiting for you when you are done with this practice.

ASSESSING YOUR PRACTICE

Using a scale of (0 to 5), rate how difficult this practice was for you?

○ ○ ○ ○ ○

If this practice was difficult for you, make a brief list of why you think it was difficult.

....
....
....
....

If your mind wandered to other thoughts that distracted you, what were they? List them.

....
....
....
....

If your mind wandered to judgmental thoughts about this practice, what were they?

....
....
....
....

If there were any environmental distractions, what were they (noise outside, temperature, etc)?

....
....
....
....

If you practiced letting go of distractions, list how you noticed and described these distractions, or how you worked at staying present and engaged.

....
....
....
....

When will you commit to yourself to engage in this practice again?

....
....
....
....

Exercise Two:
AWARENESS AND ATTENTION TO YOUR ENVIRONMENT

Now that you have a little experience with a specific mindfulness exercise, let's expand your practice a bit. In this exercise you will again want to have a place to sit, setting aside other activities just for a few minutes. In this exercise you will again practice belly breathing, with your eyes closed, so definitely don't try and practice this while driving!

Breathe: This time, as you close your eyes and begin with three gentle breaths — in through your nose and out through your mouth — settle in and focus on your breath while letting your awareness slowly expand to your environment.

Notice: Allow your awareness to take in all that you experience in your environment as you breathe. Sounds from within the room where you sit, such as the sounds of a ticking clock, the sounds of an air conditioner or heater, and notice what you experience regarding the temperature of the room or the firmness of the chair that holds you. Notice any smells that come into your nose such as air freshener, dust, incense, whatever is present.

Allow your awareness to take in sounds that come in from other rooms or just outside your room, such as the sound of people talking, children playing, wind or traffic, whatever it is that you are aware of through your senses of hearing, smell and touch.

Let the sounds, smells or physical feelings just come and go, perhaps lingering a little while on one, and then allow other sensations into your awareness.

Describe: Describe what you hear, smell or sense with your body again, factually and without judging any of them as good or bad, just the facts. You may say to yourself, "I hear the ticking sound of a clock," or, "The sound of children playing has just entered my awareness." You may say to yourself, "I notice the smell of spring," or "I smell lilacs." Don't think of these things as distractions, rather let these sensations come and go, not holding onto them for very long, nor pushing them away too quickly.

Engage With Presence: Staying where you are in your room, sitting in your chair, be present and engaged with this practice, not letting your mind wander to other places. If you notice your attention drifting to other thoughts about anything other than your practice, just notice those thoughts, saying to yourself, "My mind has wandered away from my practice," and then bring yourself back to your practice, turning your attention toward your breath to bring you back to this moment and this practice.

One Thing: Stay with this practice, not letting anything distract you for these few minutes. At the very moment of your practice, engage in *only* this practice. Staying with your practice you are taming your mind and increasing your control over your thoughts.

ASSESSING YOUR PRACTICE

Using a scale of (0 to 5), rate how difficult this practice was for you?

○ ○ ○ ○ ○

If this practice was difficult for you, make a brief list of why you think it was difficult.

....
....
....
....

If your mind drifted from your room and the moment you practiced, describe where it went (e.g., worried about bills, thoughts about the past, etc.).

....
....
....
....

If your mind wandered to judgmental thoughts about this practice, what were they?

....
....
....
....

If there were any distractions that interfered with your practice, what were they?

....
....
....
....

If you noticed that you drifted from this practice, describe how you worked at staying present and engaged (e.g., using your breath to come back, etc.).

....
....
....
....

When will you commit to yourself to engage in this practice again?

....
....
....
....

✱ *in* Summary

In this chapter you have reviewed and started to practice mindfulness. All the other exercises will require you to be **attentive and decided** as you practice them. Whether you are practicing relationship skills or changing harmful behaviors, you will be more effective as you do this in full awareness.

Worksheet:
STATES OF MIND - BE MINDFUL

WHAT IS MINDFULNESS?

Mindfulness is a state of active, open attention on the present. When you're mindful, you observe your thoughts and feelings from a distance, without judging them as good or bad. Instead of letting your life pass you by, mindfulness means living in the moment and awakening to experience.

STATES OF MIND

EMOTIONAL MIND   **Wise Mind**   REASONABLE MIND
(OR MINDFULNESS)

EMOTIONAL MIND BEHAVIORS

are controlled by emotions and impulse. Often described as hot and intense. Distorted facts, based on feelings, intense behaviors, high energy, what feels good at the moment.

Examples of Emotional Mind include:
- Arguing with someone over a silly disagreement
- Buying an expensive item on impulse
- Making love
- Taking a walk in the rain because you like it
- Getting mad at your child for spilling a drink

REASONABLE MIND BEHAVIORS

are controlled by logical thinking. Often described as cool and unemotional. Intellectual, logical thinking, planning, attention to facts, focused attention, problem solving.

Examples of Reasonable Mind include:
- Planning all vacation details months ahead
- Bringing a shopping list to the grocery store
- Researching the best price for something on the Internet
- Studying for a test
- Completing a crossword puzzle

Worksheet:
GETTING INTO WISE MIND

TAKE CONTROL OF YOUR MIND

Reasonable Mind:

- This is your rational, thinking, logical mind
- It plans and evaluates things logically
- It is your "cool" part
- Reasonable Mind can be very beneficial, but when taken to extremes can be very cruel and destructive

Emotional Mind:

- Emotions can be hot and intense
- Emotions can communicate quickly and influence others
- Emotions are what motivate us to action
- Emotions are what keep us attached to others and building relationships

Wise Mind:

- Wise Mind is the integration of Emotional Mind and Reasonable Mind
- You cannot overcome or control Emotional Mind with Reasonable Mind
- You must go within and integrate these two states of mind
- Peace and connection will result with synthesis of Emotional and Reasonable Mind
- Disconnection and misery will result at the extremes of Emotional Mind and Reasonable Mind

Everyone Has A Wise Mind!

- Some people have simply never experienced it.
- No one is in Wise Mind all of the time.

the take-away:
Wise Mind integrates the emotional problems with reasonable solutions.

DESCRIBE YOUR EXPERIENCES IN EACH STATE OF MIND:

Emotional Mind: *(Ex: Hot, Intense)*

....
....
....
....
....
....
....

Reasonable Mind: *(Ex: Cold, Calculated)*

....
....
....
....
....
....
....
....
....

Wise Mind:

....
....
....
....
....
....
....
....
....

Examples of extremes:

Emotional Mind: *"I feel awful."*

Reasonable Mind: (Not "reasonable" at extremes) *"It's all my fault, I should die."*

Wise Mind: *"Today is a new day. I will not always feel this way. I can figure out how to solve any of my problems."*

Worksheet:
MINDFULNESS "WHAT" SKILLS

Observe

Notice each experience, images, thoughts, sensations, movements and feelings. Both internal and external. Try not to get caught in the experience. Just observe it and let it go. To observe is simply experiencing with awareness of your feelings, thoughts and sensations directly without the use of words. Everything is connected, therefore don't get lost. Stay in the moment. Try to observe every detail of the moment. Try to see both the beauty and the chaos. Don't be a pessimist.

Describe

Describe is putting words on experience and experience into words. The ability to put verbal labels to (internal and external) events is essential for self-control. Many people rely on the help of a Therapist or good friend to describe. I can think of many times personally being overwhelmed with the emotional impact of a situation that I was able to gain clarity outside my awareness through describing in detail my situation to another trusted friend. You can also "describe" by journaling.

Participate

Participate is the skill of throwing yourself into your objectives whole-heartedly without self-consciousness. Participate is the "go for it" feeling you have when you enthusiastically pursue an activity meaningful to you. Participate is the satisfying experience of becoming absorbed completely in what you are doing. Your goal is to fully participate in life and enjoy living by letting go of any compulsions or self-defeating behavior.

✏️ **Exercise:**
MINDFULNESS "WHAT" SKILLS

Put these skills to practice.

Describe an experience when you were able to use Wise Mind by using the "What" skills. Did using the skill affect your thoughts, feelings or behaviors?

Observe
- Watch your thoughts and feelings and be aware of all connections.
- Do not push away your thoughts and feelings, just let them happen, see fully your reality.
- Focus your full attention on one thing.
- When you fully focus and allow awareness from your senses you will be able to find clarity in conflict.

....
....
....
....
....
....

Describe
- Put words on the experience. For example: "I feel sad right now" or "My stomach muscles are tightening" or "I feel sick."

....
....
....
....
....
....

Participate
- Become one with your experience: Fully experience your feelings without being self-conscious.

....
....
....
....
....
....

Worksheet:
MINDFULNESS "HOW" SKILLS

Non-Judgmentally

The goal of non-judgmentally is to see things from non-polarized perspectives. Flexibility of thinking is characterized by the ability to entertain other points of view. Consider, too, how you would think about something if you were feeling better. Strive to be factual and unglue your opinions from the facts. You could try to see things from someone else's point of view. Instead of polarized extremes, activate your Wise Mind to find balance, unity and acceptance.

- Don't evaluate. Just the facts.
- Accept the moment.
- Acknowledge the emotion.

One - Mindfully

Do one thing at a time. Do not multi-task. It is proven to be much more effective to give your full attention to doing just one thing with all of your focus.

- Concentrate your mind. Do one thing at a time.
- Let go of distractions and give your undivided attention.
- Thinking of one thing at a time decreases anxiety.

Effectively

A skill is an ability acquired by training. As you learn and refine skills, you become more effective, i.e., you are able to maximize positive outcomes and minimize negative outcomes. In familiar situations, you know how to maximize benefits because you know from experience what works. But in unfamiliar or difficult situations, when you don't have the benefit of previous experience, you need skills to guide you to the best possible outcome.

- Focus on what works.
- Play by the rules. All of the rules. Do not lie or cheat.
- Keep your eye on what you want in the long run.
- Let go of anger. Anger and vengeance hurts you and doesn't work.

the take-away:
Meet the situation you are in by focusing on what you can control. Practice *radical acceptance* with your mistakes. This will help you learn and grow.

 Exercise:
MINDFULNESS "HOW" SKILLS

Put these skills to practice.

Describe the experience when you were able to use wise mind by using the "how" skills. Did using the skill affect your thoughts feelings or behaviors?

Non-Judgmentally

....
....
....
....
....
....

One-Mindfully

....
....
....
....
....
....

Effectively

....
....
....
....
....
....

Worksheet:
RECOGNIZING DIALECTICAL DILEMMAS

Many times you experience dialectical dilemmas or "opposites" at the same time. *For example, emotional vulnerability is often associated with self-invalidation.* When you are at these extremes, you must search for balance. Destructive behaviors will only make the emotional extremes worse.

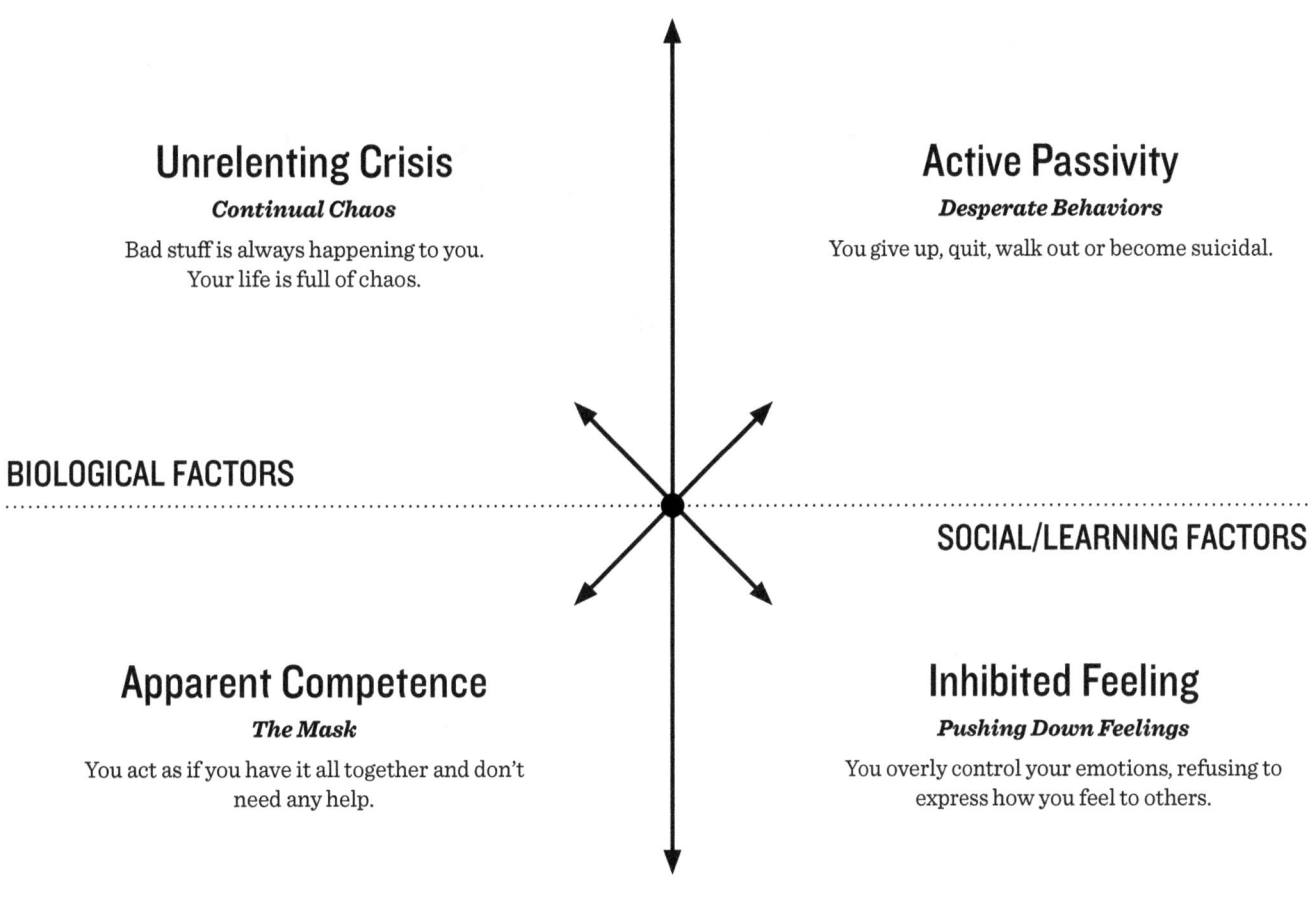

Emotional Vulnerability
Intense misery, sadness or shame over something or someone you really care about.

Unrelenting Crisis
Continual Chaos
Bad stuff is always happening to you. Your life is full of chaos.

Active Passivity
Desperate Behaviors
You give up, quit, walk out or become suicidal.

BIOLOGICAL FACTORS

SOCIAL/LEARNING FACTORS

Apparent Competence
The Mask
You act as if you have it all together and don't need any help.

Inhibited Feeling
Pushing Down Feelings
You overly control your emotions, refusing to express how you feel to others.

Self-Invalidation
You're Not Worthy
You blame yourself for your misery and become extremely sensitive to any perceived criticism from others.

Chapter VI

CRISIS SURVIVAL SKILLS

The Reality Of Emotional Pain

One fact of life that you are all too familiar with is that of the presence of emotional pain. Emotional pain is simply inescapable. Life will be filled with its share of loss and disappointment, and this is true for all of us. This doesn't mean that it should be easy for you, nor is this to say that your problems are not of any significance.

Say "yes" to your life, face your pain skillfully and refuse to live in a state of perpetual misery. Remember, it's all a matter of attention and focus.

Where are your eyes looking?

Actually, they are of *great* significance and how you respond to your pain can, in many cases, mean the difference between life and death, and make a great difference between suffering in misery and having the **life that you want**.

Your intense emotional pain may have battered you for a good part of your life, but the skills you are about to practice are going to help you change those feelings of helplessness.

These skills are designed specifically with emotional pain and crises in mind. They are practical, concrete and simple enough to be practiced even in a strong storm of emotional pain.

What you will need to bear in mind as you begin learning these crisis survival skills is that first of all, **pain is a fact of life**, and secondly, you can learn to respond to your pain differently. You will, with time and practice, find yourself **responding more skillfully** to situations that evoke powerful emotional pain. You will not be able to avoid pain or eradicate it from your life — that's the bad news in all of this.

But the good news is you don't have to be helpless or fragile when you face it.

SUFFERING IS OPTIONAL

When we begin to teach skills to our clients, we commonly hear that we don't know what our clients are going through, that we don't know how hard it is for them to face the storms of emotional pain in their lives.

And you know what?

They're right. We don't know *exactly* what it's like for them facing their loneliness as they do, or dealing with their histories.

But we *do* know our own pain, loss, fear and struggles, and that makes for a little common ground between us and our clients. And the other thing that we know is that we have many clients who, over the course of treatment, come to see how well the skills do work when clients use them again and again and again, not giving up in the face of pain or despite occasional setbacks or lapses into old patterns.

What we have learned from our clients is that these skills make a great difference between pain and suffering. Pain is something that we're all stuck with, experiencing and responding to it in our respective ways, but **suffering is optional**.

This experience of emotional suffering will arise when there is a failure to accept reality as it is, and on its own terms. Suffering will arise when pain is not acknowledged as pain.

Suffering arises when emotional pain is held on to, and we fix our attention on it; and where our attention is, there is also the direction of our hearts and minds.

As powerful principles for your practice of these crisis survival skills, you will need to adopt an outlook of **willingness and acceptance**, using your mindfulness skills to do so, saying to yourself that your pain is your pain, nothing more than that, and nothing less. Hating your pain, rejecting your pain, or willfully trying to rescind reality, is akin to self-invalidation.

If you focus your attention and your energy on wishing you were not facing the things you are, you do not have your attention and your energy turned towards facing your pain. Whether you willingly accept the pain and choose to respond to it with acceptance and the practice of these skills, or willfully turn toward rejecting reality, the pain will still be present.

Willfully rejecting the situations that cause you pain, and the real presence of your painful emotions, will likely amplify your pain, and then you will have the company of misery, or what we have been calling suffering.

So now, it's time to adopt willingness, which is an approach to your life where you are engaged, and you live in your life from one moment to the next, neither trying to control reality, (and who hasn't tried?), nor is it the practice of being overly passive as though you are a spectator without influence.

We will have more to say on willingness and willfulness in upcoming pages. This is something that you can do, just as our clients that we have worked with have done — even as they have faced many of the same challenges that you face.

✏️ Exercise:
getting ready:
An Exercise For Preparation

Using the following questionnaire, take some time to think about what's challenging about facing your emotional pain, and why it's difficult to do so. Understanding and validating these dynamics will help you to recognize them as obstacles.

And remember, as long as you are aware of them, you can overcome your obstacles

What situations would you say are the most difficult for you to face?

Use the following list as possible ideas that might fit the problem exactly, checking all that apply, or use them as ways to get yourself thinking about other problems and situations, and write those out in the "other" space.

- ○ Divorce or relationship breakup
- ○ Being told I'm too emotional when I express myself
- ○ Being reprimanded or criticized
- ○ Thinking about a past hurt or wrong
- ○ Remembering or thinking about a loss
- ○ Being stood up for a date or an appointment
- ○ Thinking about when I let someone else down
- ○ Thinking about how I've hurt others
- ○ Getting fired from a job or thinking about when I was fired
- ○ Believing I'm unlovable
- ○ Suspecting someone else of disliking me
- ○ Letting my bills fall behind
- ○ Having an intense argument with someone
- ○ Dealing with legal matters
- ○ When I think that someone will abandon me
- ○ Feeling lonely, sad, angry or fearful

Other(s):

....
....
....

When you're faced with a painful situation, what would you say has been your typical response?

Use the following checklist as a way to identify some of those patterns, and use the "other" space to write in those that are not listed.

- ○ I overeat or binge eat
- ○ I drink too much coffee or alcohol
- ○ I injure myself
- ○ I spend money I don't have or go on shopping sprees
- ○ I think about killing myself
- ○ I tell others that I'm going to kill myself
- ○ I use drugs or abuse my prescription drugs
- ○ I make extreme demands of others
- ○ I call other people too much
- ○ I focus on how horrible everything is
- ○ I focus on how horrible I am, or hate myself
- ○ I smoke, or smoke more than usual (binge smoking)
- ○ I don't go to work or school
- ○ I avoid other people

Other(s):

....
....
....

Do you have any thoughts or fears about trying to change that may be obstacles?

What are they? Use the following checklist to identify any that match, and use the "other" space to write them out if you don't see a close match on the list.

- ○ I don't know what else to do
- ○ I worried that I will try to change and fail
- ○ Other people won't support me
- ○ Other people will get in the way of my efforts
- ○ My current methods for dealing with my pain work fairly well
- ○ Change sounds like a lot of work
- ○ I don't know where to start
- ○ I'm not sure that in the heat of a crisis I'll be able to think straight
- ○ I've tried to change in the past and haven't
- ○ My pain is too much to do anything about
- ○ I really don't see the point right now

Other(s):
....
....
....

What do you have to gain by responding differently to your emotional pain?

Use the checklist to help you identify those, and use the "other" space to list reasons that are not there.

- ○ I can become stronger and more resilient
- ○ I can increase my self-respect
- ○ I can spend my energy solving my problems
- ○ I can *ask* others for help instead of demanding it

- ○ I can improve my relationships
- ○ I will be able to stand my pain
- ○ I can stop living in misery
- ○ I will be able to accept myself
- ○ I will begin to take my own problems seriously by facing them
- ○ I can spend my time and energy on constructive tasks or enjoyable activities
- ○ I will be healthier by not hurting myself
- ○ Others will respect me more and see how capable I am of facing my pain
- ○ I do better at work or school

Other(s):

....
....
....

TOLERATING EMOTIONAL PAIN

This chapter and the exercises within it will address your challenges regarding tolerating emotional pain. Now that we have established that pain is an inevitable part of your life, we are turning toward the "how's" of tolerating emotional pain.

Tolerating emotional pain is not just a matter of "sucking it up," or denying that your emotions are powerful, especially negative emotions, since that would be a practice in both invalidation and futility.

Tolerating emotional pain will require acceptance and your ongoing practice of your mindfulness skills in awareness, engaging with presence and then taking deliberate action to interrupt these powerful emotional states, at least taking the edge off them so that you can more effectively and deliberately choose a course of action that will prevent crises from occurring, likely end with you not making a bad situation worse, and surviving crises if they do occur.

Naturally, tolerance means that you will experience powerful negative experiences. As you face these emotions and situations that prompt them, you will begin to develop an increased tolerance for them, reducing somewhat, the threshold of pain that you experience.

Since you experience these emotions anyway, you have to learn to relate with them differently, and one element of learning to relate to them differently will require that you engage in challenging distorted thoughts (not *wrong*, but distorted) about what these emotions and their surrounding situations truly mean. Another element of the practice of these skills in your process of change will require that you engage in a kind of **exposure therapy**.

What Is Exposure Therapy?

Exposure therapy is usually a treatment for anxiety disorders, posttraumatic stress disorder (PTSD), or phobias.

If you have ever heard of someone overcoming their overwhelming fear of something, say social gatherings (a fear which blocks your connection with other people and social functions), the phobic persons would be asked to do more of what they fear in order to reduce their fear of social gatherings.

As they approach, rather than avoid, social gatherings, the socially-anxious person would engage in **challenging their thoughts** about the gathering.

In other words, they would **face their thoughts** about perhaps embarrassing themselves, or thinking that their racing heart means they are going to have a heart attack, or the possibility of "freaking out" in front of the other people.

They would also engage in breathing to help reduce their anxiety as they approached social gatherings.

They might begin their exposure by first meeting with a friend, or going to a job interview, and then slowly increase their exposure to larger gatherings, perhaps with a friend at first, and then by themselves. Eventually, this person would come to feel more comfortable at social gatherings as they became more tolerant of these situations, and they notice their anxiety in these situations diminishing over time. In many cases, the person learns to effectively manage their anxiety as they widen their social world and functioning.

In your case, with respect to powerful negative emotions and crises, your exposure to your emotions, through awareness and with the practice of the upcoming skills, you will become less emotionally-phobic and less crisis-phobic. The issues will likely continue to make you feel uncomfortable to a degree, but as you gradually gain mastery of your new skills, you will find that you can handle them. You will discover that, indeed, you can survive both your emotions and your crises. You will become more tolerant of them.

saying "yes" to your life: Cultivating Willingness

As you have already begun practicing many of the skills in this book, you no doubt have already been willing, or have exercised a degree of willingness. That is to say, you have already said **"yes" to acceptance and change**, and you have said "yes" to engagement of your practice.

But still, what is willingness?

Willingness is related to acceptance, and is the practice of adopting an outlook turning your will toward facing the situations that you face just as they are. Willingness is participating in your life, even in dire circumstances, to do what you can to change the things that you can, and to accept those things you cannot change. It's a decision to engage in new behaviors that eventually become new patterns, to have a **new way of living in your life** as only you can live it.

Willingness lets you accept the rain and the sunshine, the night and the day; willingness lets you accept that **your life has beauty in it**, just as it has its share of misery. Willingness is the practice of flexibility of thought and behavior, and relating to others.

You are now probably realizing the relationship of willingness not only to acceptance, but also the process of dialectics that goes beyond the ineffectual either/or stance toward your life.

For the upcoming skills you will need to be willing to try them out since, at first glance, they may seem ridiculous to you, and they will seem ridiculous if you cling to judgments.

Before we introduce them, we also want to say that these skills are offered because they are behaviors that have been looked at by researchers of emotions who have found that persons who engage in these behaviors, whether intuitively or because they were taught these behaviors, are less impulsive and demonstrate an ability to engage effectively in relevant activities even when they feel their negative emotions.

So, with your adoption of **willingness to learn and practice** these new skills, we proceed.

CRISIS SURVIVAL SKILLS

Self-Soothe:

To soothe, you will engage your senses, using touch, smell, sight, sound and taste in ways that counteract your intense emotional states. For example, using touch and smell together, you might apply a skin lotion to your hands or other parts of your body. The feel of lotion can be soothing, and if you pick a lotion that also has a fragrance that you enjoy, the scent of the lotion will add to your soothing. Visually, you might look at flowers, art books with prints of calming landscapes or other beautiful images. To soothe yourself aurally, or with sound, you might listen to soft jazz music, or slower classical pieces. With your sense of taste you can chew a piece of gum with peppermint or another flavor that you find relaxing, eat a small portion of a favorite food or beverage (we recommend non-alcoholic) that contains soothing flavors.

Use Strong Sensations:

You can also engage in behaviors that interrupt urges that come with these powerful emotions, as well as interrupt impulsive behavioral patterns that make bad situations worse. For example, you can induce intense sensations in your body that interrupt urges for self-destructive behaviors. You can clench ice cubes for as long as you can take it, take a very cold bath or shower, or bite into lemon wedges.

Distract:

Distractions can serve to derail your focus from rumination on your emotional pain or thoughts like, "I may as well give in. What's the point in trying to do better?"

Distractions include anything that can really get your attention, and override self-condemnation, or other intrusive thoughts. For example, you might read or work a puzzle. If that's not enough, then perhaps exercise will be. Or mowing the yard. Anything at all that can take your mind away from crisis-focused thinking.

 **Exercise:**

next steps: **Preparing For Crises**

THE IMPORTANCE OF PREPARATION

You are about to make your crisis "emergency kit." Just as you need to carry a spare tire in the trunk of your car for that unexpected flat tire moment, your crisis emergency kit will be a handy collection of items and strategies that you will prepare now, **prior to crises**, as tools ready to use immediately if/when you are faced with your next crisis.

MAKING YOUR EMERGENCY KIT

The following is a guide to making your emergency kit. You will also need to make sure that you have access to each of the things you put in your emergency kit.

For example, if you plan to use clutching ice cubes as a way of interrupting urges, then you will need to make sure that you at least have an ice tray, and even consider putting a few ice cubes into several individual sandwich bags which can be readily accessed without having to scramble in the heat of the moment. That might be your kitchen emergency kit, or one of several kits for home.

If you plan to use self-soothing, do you have soft music, lotions or aroma therapy items? You may need to purchase some of these items.

STEP 1: REVIEW AND LIST

To include in my Emergency Kit:
1) ....
2) ....
3) ....
4) ....
5) ....
6) ....

Items I will need:
1) ....
2) ....
3) ....
4) ....
5) ....
6) ....

Locations for my emergency kit(s) (home, school, travel):

1) ....
2) ....
3) ....
4) ....
5) ....
6) ....

STEP 2: MAKING YOUR CRISIS KIT(S)

*Remember to gather a list of phone numbers of supportive people who can help you in a crisis.

Now that you have reviewed and made your lists of what you will use for future crises and you know what content you will include, as well as where you keep these items, your next step is to actually create the kit(s). How will you make your kit(s)?

It doesn't need to be fancy. You can keep these very simple, using boxes, purses, baskets, bags or closets and cabinets. Here are some examples of kits made by clients we have treated in the past to give you some ideas to get you going on your own.

💼 Kit 1:

Description: Ice cubes in plain or ziplock sandwich bags, at least two with four or five ice cubes.
Where: Kitchen freezer at home.
Why: For potential crises that may arise when at home and to interrupt strong urges for self-harm.

💼 Kit 2:

Description: Small cardboard box containing two bottles of hand lotions. One scented with lavender, the second lilac, and my iPod. One large sticky note posted on box labeled "soothe kit."
Where: At home on bed stand.
Why: To soothe when anxiety mounts at bedtime, helping to bring calm.

 Kit 3:

Description: Small rubber/plastic food container filled with a small bag of super sour candies.
Where: Workplace.
Why: To interrupt powerful negative emotions that sometimes occur at work, helping to stay present and effective at work.

You're probably getting the idea now. After you make your crisis kit(s) and strategically position them, you will use the following exercises, not only when you feel a crisis mounting, but when you begin to feel strong negative emotions, before the crisis mounts. This is a good way to practice so that you can be ready for anything substantial that might come up. We strongly recommend that you do the following exercise after you construct your kit or two, so that you can rehearse and record your results.

✏ Exercise:
CRISIS SURVIVAL

1) Describe the crisis or stressful situation:
....
....
....
....

2) List the emotions that you experienced:
....
....
....
....

3) List the thoughts you had as the situation was happening:
....
....
....
....

4) List the action urges you experienced:
....
....
....
....

5) List the self-soothe skills that you practiced:

....
....
....
....

6) List the outcomes or results of the action you took, including whether the situation was better, worse or stayed the same:

....
....
....
....

7) List other factors affecting your mood and emotions (lack of sleep, illness, missed medicines, pressure, etc.):

....
....
....
....

8) How will you prepare better for the next crisis or stressful situation?

....
....
....
....

 Exercise:
POST-CRISIS ASSESSMENT

As has become our usual practice throughout the course of this book, this exercise continues to widen and sharpen your awareness to the important details that occur during a crisis that can be overlooked if it is not combed through afterwards.

This way, you can identify steps toward or away from willingness, your effective engagement of the skills, and how to become even more effective next time. Make photocopies of the actual worksheet for yourself so that you may use it repeatedly, as often as you need to. Use the following worksheet to analyze a recent crisis.

1) Identify the crisis (include emotions, and thoughts):

....
....
....
....

2) Identify the trigger or triggers:

....
....
....
....

3) Identify your behavior or actions. What did you do?

....
....
....
....

4) Identify any skills you implemented, and if you didn't identify, why not?

....
....
....
....

5) Identify any target behaviors you may have engaged in (threats, fits, self-harm):

....
....
....
....

6) Identify the consequences or outcomes:

....
....
....

7) Identify how well this course of action worked for you:

....
....
....
....

8) Identify any secondary "fallout" from this situation:

....
....
....
....

9) Identify how you will be even better prepared for the next time (new skills, willingness):

....
....
....
....

✏ Exercise:
IN-THE-MOMENT GUIDE

Imagine right now you are experiencing a crisis. It will be important for you to give your full attention to the following instructions, giving all of your commitment to try the skills at this moment. The aim of this exercise is not to radically change your life or make the pain you experience right now go away forever, but to help you tolerate your emotional pain skillfully, mindfully, focusing on effective outcomes to getting through this situation without making it worse, while continuing to move toward the life you are building with your skills.

DO THIS NOW!

1) *Pause right now!* Take three centering and calming breaths as you approach this exercise.

....
....
....
....

2) Describe the crisis, writing it out here. Use descriptive and factual language as opposed to judgmental language:

....
....
....
....

3) Describe your emotions, factually and descriptively, using your observation skills from mindfulness:

....
....
....
....

4) Describe your thoughts, factually and descriptively, not getting caught up in them, nor taking them as facts, but as thoughts about facts in your situation:

....
....
....
....

5) Describe what kind of action urges you have right now. Are there urges to harm yourself, binge eat, take a shopping spree?

....
....
....
....

6) Use the following suggestions to list skills you can use in this moment to effectively manage your urges and behaviors: Soothing (taste, smell, sound, vision, and touch)?

....
....
....
....

7) *Pause right now!* Take THREE MORE BREATHS, bring your attention back to this moment, and stay in this moment without resorting to your target behaviors.

....
....
....
....

8) Use this checklist to check all the positive outcomes you have to look forward to if you use your skills and deny your target behaviors.

☐ Increased self-respect

☐ Mastery over my new skills

☐ Increased tolerance for strong negative emotions

☐ Potential to eliminate dangerous impulsive behaviors

☐ Enhanced relationships with others

Add your own:

....
....
....

With every practice of each exercise, you will become more skillful at managing your crises.

 Exercise:

TAKING ACTION IN THE MOMENT

Keep a copy of this worksheet in a place where it will be easy for you to get to in the moment of a crisis, and put a bookmark or sticky note tab on this page so that you can easily reference this worksheet. Follow the simple steps here:

Step 1: Describe what triggered your current crisis?

....
....
....
....

Step 2: Describe what your emotions, thoughts and urges are right now?

....
....
....
....

Step 3: List your options for effective action. What can you do RIGHT NOW?

....
....
....
....

Step 4: Take action to self-soothe or distract from the intense emotion!

....
....
....
....

Soothe: To soothe myself, I can:

....
....
....
....

Distract: I can distract myself with:

....
....
....
....

MIND TRICKS

PUT YOUR THOUGHTS ON A SHELF

Use your imagination as you put your distressing, crisis-related thoughts into boxes. Put anxious thoughts into a hypothetical box, and then put that box up on a shelf, leaving it there for the time being. Do the same with thoughts about harming yourself, thoughts about people mistreating you, your judgments and emotionally-charged thoughts.

LIST YOUR THOUGHTS

As you feel the urgency of the crisis coming on, sit down and make a brief list of your thoughts, worries and concerns. Make it as long as it has to be. After completing the list, either file it or put it in a drawer. You can take the list out at another time when the crisis has dissipated. Then make another list of **effective action** you can take to solve your problems.

ATTEND TO YOUR BREATH

As you feel distress and crisis mounting, pause, sit down in a chair, close your eyes, and begin to breathe deeply. Focus only on your breathing for as long as you can. If your mind wanders back to thoughts about how awful everything is, just notice that your mind has wandered. Pause, and take another breath, bringing your focus back to your breath.

LET GO OF JUDGMENTS

Let go of judgments about how hard it is to maintain your focus on your breath. Set a goal for yourself to stay engaged in this practice for 35 minutes, take a break, and then come back to it, again and again, as you slowly and surely **gain more control** over your focus.

✱ *in* Summary

In closing this chapter, we want to say: *keep at it*. Use these skills over and over again and you will find yourself continuing to build mastery over your actions in difficult moments of crisis. We suggest that you make copies of the worksheets so that you can use them over and over again, as often as you need them.

In our next chapter we will be looking at emotions and how they work for you, and how they can work against you. Many of the principles and skills in that chapter will enhance your understanding and practice of crisis survival skills as you continue your journey toward effective living.

Worksheet:
SELF-SOOTHE TO COUNTERACT INTENSE EMOTION

Remember these skills with **"5 SENSES"**

SEE • HEAR • SMELL • TASTE • TOUCH

Engage your senses in ways that counteract your intense emotional states.

For example, using touch and smell together, you might apply lotion to your body. The feel of the lotion is soothing to your skin (touch) and the good fragrance (smell) adds to the soothing experience.

You might look at flowers, art books, majestic landscape or any beautiful image (see), and listen to soft jazz or classical music (hear) to enhance the calming properties.

Chew a piece of flavorful gum or eat some of your favorite foods or beverage (non-alcoholic) that contains soothing flavors.

Step outside and listen to the sounds of nature. Birds chirping, train whistle in the distance, airplane flying overhead. Feel the light breeze blowing through your hair.

Add movement to self-soothe. Dance, run, rock, sway, tap, squeeze your hands together. Movement is inherently soothing.

Treat yourself WELL by engaging your senses through an enjoyable experience.

Adapted from skills Training Manual for Treating Borderline Personality Disorder By Marsha Linehan. ©1993 The Guilford Press

✏️ Exercise:
now, you do it.
PRACTICE USING THE "5 SENSES" SKILL.

Practice this skill to soothe yourself and counteract intense emotion.

In what situation did you use this skill?
....
....
....
....

Did using the skill help you to avoid conflict or cope with uncomfortable feelings?
....
....
....
....

Describe what activity you did and what senses you used.
....
....
....
....

How long did it take before you felt like your intense emotion was subsiding?
....
....
....
....

Worksheet:
MAKE IMPROVEMENT EVERY DAY

Remember these skills with **"IMPROVE"**

Imagery
Use your imagination to create a relaxing fantasy to let your mind go.

Meaning
Create purpose, value and meaning in your life.

Prayer
Let God or a higher being give you stength to bear any pain.

Relaxation
Listen to a relaxation podcast, take a bath, breathe deeply, relax your body.

One Thing in the Moment
Focus your mind to stay in the moment that you are in.

Vacation
Give yourself a brief vacation. Take a breather from work.

Encouragement
Be your own cheerleader. "I can do it!"

Adapted from skills Training Manual for Treating Borderline Personality Disorder By Marsha Linehan. ©1993 The Guilford Press

✏️ Exercise:
now, you do it.
PRACTICE USING THE "IMPROVE" SKILL.

Practice this skill and see overall improvement in balancing your life.

How did you use this skill?
....
....
....
....

Did this skill help you in a crisis situation or did you find it helpful in maintaining a healthy balance?
....
....
....
....

Is there a part of the skill you don't understand or need clarity on?
....
....
....
....

How often do you find yourself working on this skill?
....
....
....
....

Worksheet:
CRISIS SURVIVAL SKILLS

Remember these skills with the term **"ACCEPTS"**

Activities
Engage in a healthy activity that will cause a distraction, such as exercise or a hobby.

Contributing
Do something for someone else, such as a thoughtful gesture for a friend or volunteering.

Comparisons
Focus on people or events that are worse off than yourself. Such as the homeless or disasters.

Emotions
Let yourself experience any emotion. Listen to a happy song or watch a dramatic movie.

Push Away
Push away situations that are bothering you. Temporarily ignore and avoid them.

Thoughts
Try something that will make you use your mind such as reading, puzzles or games.

Sensations
Experience a semi-intense sensation. For example hold ice in your hand or put a heat pad on your back, or eat something sour like a lemon.

The Key Is To Distract
This skill uses distractions to take your mind away from the crisis-focused thinking.

Adapted from skills Training Manual for Treating Borderline Personality Disorder By Marsha Linehan. ©1993 The Guilford Press

✏️ Exercise:
now, you do it.
PRACTICE USING THE "ACCEPTS" SKILL.

Practice this skill to get through a crisis situation without harming yourself.

In what situation did you use this skill?

....
....
....
....

Did using the skill help you to avoid conflict or cope with uncomfortable feelings?

....
....
....
....

Which area was the most difficult for you to do?

....
....
....
....

What might you do differently next time to improve your use of the skill?

....
....
....
....

✏️ Exercise:
LISTING PROS AND CONS

Make a list of the pros and cons of tolerating distress. And a pro and cons list of acting on impulses.

Coping by hurting yourself, abusing alcohol or drugs, or doing something else impulsive is destructive. Focus on your long-term goals. There is light at the end of the tunnel. **Pain is temporary.** Think of times when pain has subsided.

Think of the negative consequences of not tolerating your current distress. Remember what has happened in the past when you have acted impulsively to escape the moment. Did you improve or did it cause further pain?

Think of the positive consequences of tolerating the distress. Imagine how good you will feel when you achieve your goals and don't act impulsively. You can do it! Use the DBT skills and you can overcome!

	Resisting Impulses	**Acting on Impulses**
PROS		
CONS		

Remember to consider short-term and long-term pros and cons. When in emotional mind, focus on the pros of resisting the impulse and the cons of acting on the impulse. Once you have made a decision focus your mind on the positives regarding the decision you've made and the negatives of not making that decision. Give your mind a place to rest.

Chapter VII

HOW EMOTIONS WORK

Emotions bring great bliss and enjoyment in addition to deep agony and despair. If you have BPD, you can probably relate more with the latter.

The first step toward a **brighter future** is reclaiming control of your emotional well-being, and ultimately your life. Make a commitment to understand and to relate differently with your emotional pain. **Deal with it head on, eyes open, with mindfulness.** Know that taking on the task to change your emotional life requires courage and commitment to yourself.

We sincerely hope you decide to make this critical commitment based on a growing hope, acceptance and compassion for yourself. Your personal commitment to life brings you closer to working your way out of emotional suffering and creating a life you find worth living.

In this chapter we are going to discuss how your emotions work, talk more about why persons with BPD are so emotionally sensitive and reactive, and how you can skillfully change your emotional states with mindfulness and emotion-congruent actions.

Also we will discuss how to increase your emotional resilience so that you are less vulnerable to strong emotional states when your emotions *are* triggered.

Take a moment to do a little exploration of your current understanding of emotions, including messages about emotions that you received from your family and environment.

This next exercise in awareness-building will prepare you for the exercises in changing your ideas about — and your relationship with — your emotions.

✏️ Exercise:
YOUR EMOTIONAL HERITAGE

Describe your family's emotional style, as you remember it growing up (repressive, gregarious or free?).

....
....
....
....

Did you grow up feeling safe to express your emotions? Explain why or why not?

....
....
....
....

Describe any implicit, or unspoken, messages you received from your family regarding the expression of emotions.

....
....
....
....

Describe how your parents, or caregivers, expressed their emotions as you grew up.

....
....
....
....

Describe how you think this affected your understanding of your emotions?

....
....
....
....

✏️ Exercise:
EXPLORING YOUR BELIEFS ABOUT EMOTIONS

Exercise: *Using the following checklist, check all the items that ring true for you regarding your beliefs about your emotions and emotions in general.* For each one that you check, try to provide a brief rationale for why you hold that belief or explain where you think you got that message, such as, "this is what my family taught me," or "this is what I saw growing up," or "because others disapproved of emotional expressions" or "people think you're weird if you're emotional."

Try to answer as you truly believe and not as you might think we want you to answer. This exercise is to benefit you, and honesty is what you need with yourself if you're to best learn the coming skills in this area.

EMOTIONS ARE TERRIBLE THINGS.

Rationale/source of belief:

....
....
....
....

SHOWING EMOTIONS IS A SIGN OF WEAKNESS.

Rationale/source of belief:

....
....
....
....

FEELING EMOTIONS IS BAD ENOUGH, EXPRESSING THEM IS WORSE.

Rationale/source of belief:

....
....
....
....

SHOWING ANGER MAKES YOU A BAD OR UNKIND PERSON

Rationale/source of belief:

....
....
....
....

IT'S BEST NOT TO TELL ANYONE HOW YOU FEEL.

Rationale/source of belief:

....
....
....
....

BEING EMOTIONAL MEANS BEING OUT OF CONTROL.

Rationale/source of belief:

....
....
....
....

TELLING OTHERS YOU FEEL BAD IS A BURDEN TO THEM.

Rationale/source of belief:

....
....
....
....

CRYING IS A SIGN THAT YOU'RE "LOSING IT."

Rationale/source of belief:

....
....
....
....

I SHOULD NEVER FEEL ANXIOUS OR AFRAID.

Rationale/source of belief:
....
....
....
....

BEING EMOTIONAL DOESN'T SOLVE ANYTHING.

Rationale/source of belief:
....
....
....
....
....

IT'S BEST TO LIVE IN YOUR HEAD.

Rationale/source of belief:
....
....
....
....

THERE'S NO POINT IN TELLING ANYONE ABOUT MY FEELINGS; THEY DON'T CARE.

Rationale/source of belief:
....
....
....
....

I'M DEATHLY AFRAID TO FEEL MY EMOTIONS, THEY'RE SO POWERFUL.

Rationale/source of belief:
....
....
....
....

IF I EXPRESS MY EMOTIONS, I'LL FLY OFF THE HANDLE.

Rationale/source of belief:
....
....
....
....

I'D RATHER NOT FEEL MY EMOTIONS, THEY'RE TOO PAINFUL.

Rationale/source of belief:
....
....
....
....

From the above checklist and the preceding assessment of your emotional heritage, use the following space to summarize your current beliefs, philosophy and experience of emotions. Then you will move on to learn about how emotions work, emotional suffering and tools for changing and working with your emotions.

Your summary:
....
....
....
....
....
....
....
....
....
....
....
....
....
....
....
....
....

HOW EMOTIONS WORK

Your emotions are part of a large complex comprised of five components made up of your triggers, biology, thoughts, actions and urges. Emotions identify that something is going on with you internally or externally.

It's important to state that even though you, and many people you know, may think being emotional is a bad thing, all people are emotional; it's simply a matter of biology. And as you will see later, emotions are actually fundamentally adaptive, helping you to survive and connect to your social environment. Of course, as you know from your own experiences, emotions don't always feel adaptive. We're going to discuss that too, and what you can do about it.

Your experience of emotion is a complex system of experience, thoughts and action urges, and is a lot like standing in the rain. You may see that it is raining through a window, but you realize more fully it's raining if you step out into it and you feel the wet rain drops falling on your face and body. Emotions let you know that something is happening, inwardly or externally in your environment.

We're now going to look at five components of how emotions work.

THE FIVE COMPONENTS OF YOUR EMOTIONAL SYSTEM INCLUDE:

Triggers

Triggers are events that happen internally and externally. The trigger can be a daily event, like someone talking to you, going to work, getting a speeding ticket, or the responses of others whom you try to talk to about anything from weather to deep intimate matters.

Internal triggers may include thoughts or memories, and can fire emotional states as though these thoughts or memories are actually happening at the moment they come to mind. Whether internal or external, triggers are what set your emotions off. Here are some examples of what can trigger emotion:

Internal triggers

- Thinking about someone who criticized you
- An unpleasant or traumatic memory
- Thinking about your own shortcomings
- Ruminating on a lost relationship
- Physical pain
- Sick, hungry and tired

External triggers

- Someone gives you something you want
- Getting fired from your job or getting a new job
- You hear a strange noise outside your window at night
- Being criticized
- Violence toward you
- Discrimination

Thoughts

Your beliefs and assumptions about what is going on will be fired up as emotions take off. Thoughts that fire with emotions are usually emotion-congruent. That is to say, if you feel angry, your thoughts are likely to be angry thoughts, rigid "I'm right" thoughts, and that's normal for all people experiencing anger.

You may then have secondary thoughts about feeling angry and having angry thoughts such as "only bad mean people get angry" or "anger is wrong, I shouldn't be angry" which then can either further intensify your anger, or may even introduce a new emotional state, and also create somewhat mixed emotional experiences.

Thoughts, as mentioned above, can also set off emotion as an internal trigger. Do you think the event was positive, unfair, shameful or unbearable? These thoughts will affect your emotions. We will address thoughts in this chapter, and you can also use your skills from the chapter on thinking patterns, using refraining, thought challenges and dialectical thinking skills to work with your emotions.

A few examples of **"emotional thoughts"** include:

- Imagining smashing something when you feel angry
- Thinking you're going to fail at a task when you're anxious
- Thinking life is unfair and terrible when you feel sad
- Thinking about positive qualities of someone you love

Physical responses

Emotions, being biological and affecting heart rate, brain functioning, body language and so on, will also fire up action urges.

Your face turning red, smiling, crying, fist-clenching, wanting to hide away, are examples of immediate physical reactions you might experience during emotional states. Emotions also prepare you for action that is congruent to a specific emotion. Using anger, for example, your action tendencies will be at least somewhat aggressive, even if you don't *act* aggressively.

This is also normal for all people experiencing anger. If you feel sad, you will likely have urges to withdraw from others. In this chapter you will learn skills for becoming aware of this component of emotions, **being mindful** to what your **emotional states** are, and your urges to act, so that you can mindfully decide what will be the effective course of action.

Some examples of **physical responses** during emotional experiences include:

- Increased heart rate when you feel anxious or angry
- Decreased energy when feeling sad
- Changes in activity of neurotransmitters in your brain
- Muscular relaxation when you are experiencing love or joy

Expression

Emotions also have a role in how you communicate to others, even when you are unaware of this. This could include yelling, giving a gift to someone, staying in bed all day or complaining. Facial expressions also tend to match what someone is feeling and you may send emotional messages to others without actually saying, "I'm feeling sad." Sometimes it's hard for people with BPD to communicate effectively, frequently using incongruent body language or tone of voice to match what they are feeling.

Emotional expression also translates into how you act on your emotions. Hitting a wall sends a message that you're angry. Crying sends a message that you're sad and shaking your leg while sitting sends a message that you're feeling anxious. You'll learn skills in this chapter and in the chapter on relationship skills that help you to become a **more effective emotional communicator**.

Expression of emotion can include some of these examples:

- Smiling when you feel happy or upbeat (facial expressions)
- Verbalizing to someone how happy you are about your new job
- Slamming a door when you feel angry or frustrated (expression through action)
- Sulking and frowning when you are sad or disappointed (body language)

Fallout

Emotions have a way of lingering, sometimes even keeping themselves fired up. One indication of emotional fallout is getting stuck in the emotion. This occurs when your emotions love themselves, kind of feeding on themselves, repeating through a loop of biology, thoughts and actions while firing the same feelings over and over again.

This is a primary reason you need skills to sometimes soften emotional situations where facial expressions are not consistent with the emotions, or so you can change your body language so that the feedback loop between brain and body response shift the emotional charge, at least somewhat.

Also, some of the after-effects are that you might feel more vulnerable, or on edge, and will likely be open to having strong emotions set off by the next trigger and for this reason, **building your overall resilience** is so important.

Emotional "fallout" can also signify the results of emotion-related actions. Acting from emotions isn't always negative. Telling someone you love them when you feel love for them has the potential to make you closer to that person. Telling someone at work to stop making inappropriate advances on you might get them to stop and will actually improve the work environment for you.

Emotional fallout might have other positive effects such as getting an unexpected thank-you card from someone for something nice you did for them.

Examples of *emotional fallout* include:

- Scaring off people whom you would like closeness from
- Damaged self-respect for reactive and impulsive actions
- You may get a need met
- Lingering emotions, or emotions continuing to amplify

Chapter VIII

SO, WHAT GOOD ARE EMOTIONS ANYWAY?

We have discussed a basic outline of what is involved in the experience of emotion. Now let's talk about what good these emotions are, specifically the way in which each one is adaptive and functional, as you will see in the section on primary emotions. We will also discuss why emotions can hurt so much and examine emotional suffering, as we differentiate between primary and secondary emotions.

PRIMARY EMOTIONS

Primary emotions are the responses to events in the moment. These emotions are called **primary** because they are **basic, fundamental and adaptive**. These are emotional experiences that occur naturally through your body and brain, alerting you to activity in your environment allowing you to act accordingly to the situation at hand, and many times, without even having to think about it.

For example, you're driving to work when another driver swerves in front of you. You simply react, swerving and/or breaking to avoid a collision. At that moment when your brain and body register the possible collision, you don't need to stop and work out the physics or an algorithm in order to know what to do. You just do it and you avoid the collision. This is an example of how fear can protect you from danger.

You have a whole set of emotions that you were born with, that all of us were born with. And the good news is that emotions are just emotions. They are part of being human; common to us all. And believe it or not, the purpose of each of these emotions is to help us.

Every **primary emotion** is:

- Adaptive
- Unlearned and biologically-based
- A provider of information
- Organizing you for action
- Helpful in communication

It's because of the prior reasons that you have to learn how to relate differently to your emotions, adopting a new philosophy and core assumptions about them, and learning skills to tolerate them, change them and reduce their strength as an overwhelming force.

Below is a sample of **nine primary emotions** (not necessarily an exhaustive list) and their corresponding functions. Consider these as spectrums since emotions range in intensity.

Happiness or Joy

Feelings of happiness provide a sense of well-being and enhance your emotional resilience against stress and other negative emotional states. The good feelings that come from feeling happy and joyful are reinforcing, creating an influence that you will likely engage in the activities that produce them again and again. The good feelings suggest you should do these things again, continually approaching them. Happiness and joy stem from connectivity in relationships and engaging in fun and meaningful activities.

Love

Emotions, on the spectrum of love, range from infatuation to profound and consuming erotic love, as that between lovers and spouses, to love for friends and family. Feelings of love serve to draw you into relationships.

Anger

Physiological changes that occur when anger is triggered include increased blood flow to your arms and hands (empowering you to fight if you're in danger), a heart rate increase and a rush of hormones such as adrenaline, that creates a tremendous energy to prepare you for actions such as countering a physical attack, or overcoming a threat or obstacle blocking something that you badly want or need.

Anxiety

Anxiety, as discomforting feelings and action urges, propel you toward effective problem-solving such as at work, in order to promote the provision of needed housing and food. It can also serve as a warning that something against your wishes, wants and needs is happening, and organizes you to do something about it. If the anxiety-producing situation is resolved, the anxiety clears up and you feel better. Thus, engaging in **effective** anxiety-related behaviors are adaptive and reinforced as the uncomfortable feelings of anxiety subside as a result of these behaviors.

Disgust

Disgust signals to you that something is literally dangerous to you. As your lips distort and your nose wrinkles up, your emotions are trying to protect you from something that might be noxious, preventing you from breathing it in and certainly preventing you from eating it. Disgust is also expressed at certain ideas, morals and behaviors of yourself or others, and the face does the same thing when you think about something that disgusts you, sometimes to communicate to someone else your strong disapproval.

Fear

When fear is triggered, blood flows to the larger muscles of your body, such as your legs and arms, making it easier to take refuge from danger or flee from threats. Fear can also drain the face of color and you may freeze up for a moment, as fear prompts a quick analysis of what the best course of action will be to preserve yourself. When hormones in your brain are activated, they put you on red alert making the body "edgy" and ready for action or frozen in fear, and your focus narrows on the threat at hand.

Sadness

Sadness actually helps you to adjust to experiences of loss, say, the death of a dearly loved person or pet, or the loss of a job.

The emotion of sadness creates a drop in your energy and enthusiasm for activities that you usually find to be interesting or fun, and so positive emotions are diminished. When you feel sad you are prompted to withdraw from your normal activities and even from the company of others, taking you into an emotional space where you can consider and process the meaning of your loss.

Since your energy is low when you're deeply sorrowful, withdrawal from your normal activities seems to serve to protect you from the possibility of harm since you're more vulnerable to accidents, and on a more dire level, being taken advantage of or assaulted.

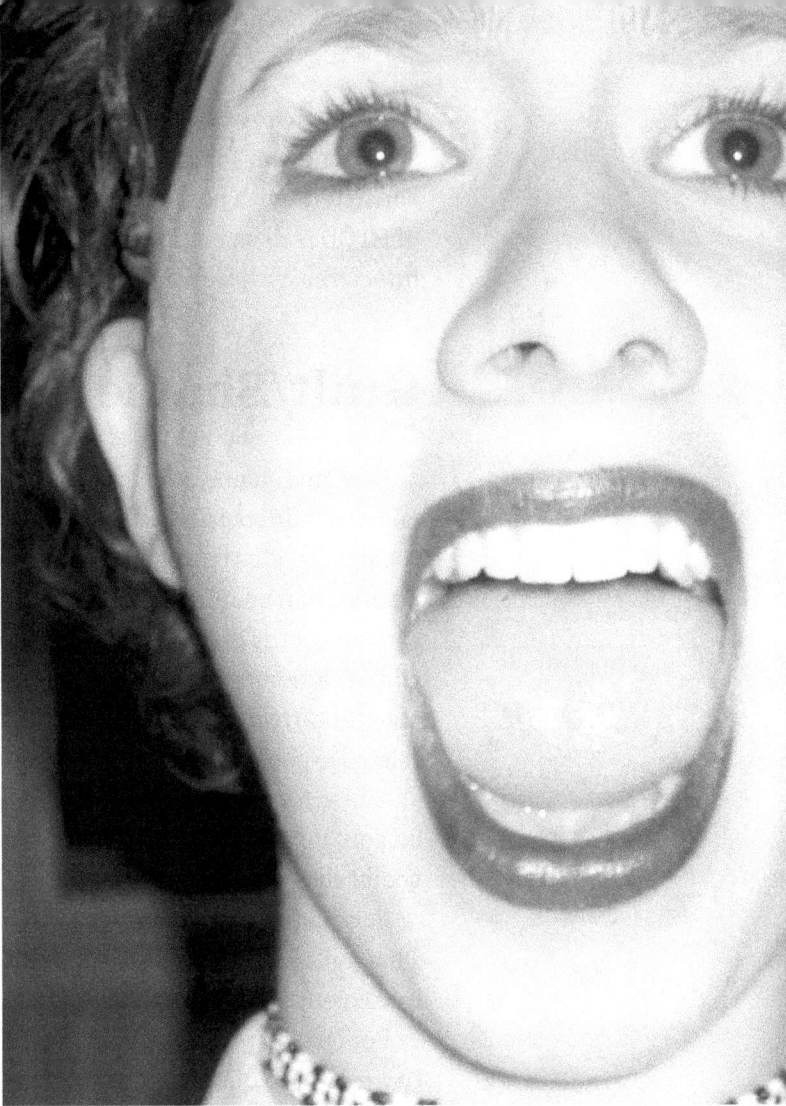

In essence, this prompting to withdraw is designed to protect you. Of course, the experience of sadness also provides important information to you about the seriousness of your loss, and to grapple with the consequences of this loss for your life.

Interest

Interest, as an emotion, draws you toward activities such as learning and exploration, as well as toward exploring relationships with other people.

As with all the primary emotions, interest has a function which is to organize you for actions related to the emotional state that sparks curiosity in a topic, person or activity. It's worth noting here that if you were unemotional, you wouldn't even be able to learn.

In fact, people who sustain head traumas that affect the emotion centers of the brain will often show a marked decrease in interest — in everything from their own relationships to learning new skills or information, and they can even forget information that was learned prior to the brain injury.

People who have experienced chronic abuse, or who have been exposed to chronic stress and fear for life, as often occurs with sexual abuse, often develop symptoms consistent with post-traumatic stress syndrome (PTSD). One of the major symptoms of PTSD is dissociation which cuts a person off from emotional experience and also interferes with learning and memory.

Guilt/Shame

Guilt and shame, as emotions, drives us to make repairs and be responsible to others and maintain socially responsible behaviors. Guilt and shame are what keep us from being sociopaths. This is a difficult emotion altogether, not just because the experience of this emotion can be intense and painful, but because of the variance of how it's discussed throughout the research and clinical world. The word "shame" is very often associated with what some refer to as "toxic" emotion. In other words, shame is considered to always be a bad thing, period, and reflects a person's basic disposition about themselves related to poor self-image.

And so for some, the word "guilt" refers to an emotional experience that corresponds to an actual mistake, offense or damage to a trust or relationship, perhaps according to social custom.

For example, you may feel guilt if you break your neighbor's window, even if by accident. That guilt may spur you to make relationship repairs, as well as reimburse them for the expense of replacing the pane.

For our purposes, we won't work too hard at making the distinction between the two except to qualify our references to this emotion as justifiable guilt/shame versus unjustified guilt/shame, the latter not corresponding to any actual wrong-doing on your part and likely a learned secondary emotional experience.

Chapter IX

SECONDARY EMOTIONS

Having established that primary emotions are fundamentally adaptive, we look at what are called **secondary emotions**, *which unlike the primary emotions, are complicated, learned, and usually not adaptive and precede episodes of behaviors targeted for change. Called secondary emotions, these emotional experiences follow the primary emotions as emotions about emotions. Secondary emotions are usually reactions to your own thoughts, or your core assumptions, and your primary emotional responses.*

WHAT ARE SECONDARY EMOTIONS?

Secondary emotions are not responses to environmental or external triggers, but reactions to the internal processes of your own thoughts and your primary emotions. This is, in part, why they are not adaptive. With secondary emotions, your focus shifts from the original trigger to your internal reactions, blocking effective action that is needed in a given moment.

Being busy with secondary emotions creates a barrier to learning to tolerate and control your primary emotional experiences, and can be considered a form of self-invalidation. It can be considered a form of self-invalidation because you are simply not acknowledging your primary emotional responses, nor addressing them as they are, on their own terms. Your primary emotional experience become muffled or muted, as they filter through your appraisal of your emotions as your enemies, or something to run and hide from. And of course without skills, and considering your history, how can it be any different?

As already mentioned, people with BPD usually have histories of having been raised in environments that invalidated their basic emotional experiences. Years of experience after experience of having their primary emotions met with indifference, or even punishment, often lead people with BPD to have conflicting information regarding their emotional experience.

On the one hand, their experience of emotion is very real to them, yet on the other hand, they are receiving a strong and constant message that these feelings, whatever they are, really don't matter, or that what they are feeling is actually wrong or bad.

COMPLICATING FACTORS

Perhaps this is your experience, having these messages deeply entrenched in your mind, feeling torn between your personal immediate experience and the messages of your environment that contradict your experience.

Chronic invalidation brainwashes you when it comes to core assumptions about emotions: primarily that they are bad and wrong, especially negative emotions. With these core assumptions deeply entrenched as your own, your primary emotional experience gets mixed up. Rather than simply *feel* the primary emotion of, say, anger, letting it serve its purpose, you interpret your experience as wrong or bad, and this in turn leads to feeling anger as a secondary emotion.

Perhaps you feel angry toward yourself for feeling what your core assumptions tell you that you shouldn't feel. Or perhaps you feel ashamed for feeling angry, or for communicating anger to someone else. In this kind of situation, you are not only feeling the primary anger, but now you are feeling secondary anger and shame, and these complicated emotions throw you off-center, making you dizzy in an emotional storm, which doesn't correspond to the original trigger or situation where you first experienced your anger.

Examples of **secondary emotional responses**:

- Feeling angry about feeling angry
- Feeling angry about feeling fear
- Feeling sad about feeling sad
- Feeling shame for feeling anxiety

✏ Exercise:
your experience of SECONDARY EMOTIONS

Use the following exercise to build your awareness of your own experiences of secondary emotions. Read each heading, and think about whether or not you have ever had an experience like this. Under each heading use the space provided to write in a brief description of the experience.

Describe a time when you ...

Felt guilty for feeling good or happy.

....
....
....
....

Felt shame for feeling angry.

....
....
....
....

Felt agitated for feeling anxious.

....
....
....
....

Felt embarrassed for feeling sad.

....
....
....
....

Felt angry for feeling fear.

....
....
....
....
....

Felt more than one emotion at once.

....
....
....
....
....

Secondary emotions usually won't help you in the adaptive way that primary emotions do, since they are further complicated by those core assumptions about emotions that turn into judgments about emotions, judgments about the situation that triggered them, and judgments about you as a person.

These secondary emotional responses cut you off from the primary emotion, robbing you of an opportunity to be informed by your emotion, to practice **tolerating your emotion**, and diverts your attention to your thoughts about the emotion and situation so that you are distracted from what originally got your emotions fired up to begin with.

EMOTIONAL SUFFERING

Individuals who suffer from BPD often describe their lives as "emotional hell," "living with emotional third-degree burns" and in terms of sheer misery.

This isn't to be taken lightly by you or mental health professionals.

A degraded quality of life due to chronic emotional suffering will foster hopelessness, not hopefulness. And for people with BPD, there is always the issue of heightened emotional sensitivity and reactivity that can instantly evolve from a tiny spark to a raging inferno — immediately, in many cases.

Emotions fire quickly and intensely, and without skills, the person with BPD is like a person surrounded by a forest fire ... with no visible path to safely exit and without firefighting equipment. The situation is alarming.

You are about to embark on a practice of learning adaptive responses to emotion, beginning the **end of your emotional suffering**, by learning emotion skills including:

- Mindfulness to emotions
- Increasing your tolerance for emotions
- Increasing your emotional resilience
- Changing your emotions

emotion skill: MINDFULNESS TO YOUR EMOTIONS

You have already begun learning about mindfulness skills. You know about noticing your thoughts and your emotions, and about describing these in factual and nonjudgmental language. Now you will build on those skills, bringing them to a narrow focus on your emotions and their triggers and fallout.

Your skills in mindfulness will assist you with becoming more observant of your primary emotional experiences, even if you have to work through the thick tangle of your secondary emotions to get there. Mindfulness will help you get unstuck from secondary emotions, and see emotions for what they are: simply emotions.

As you begin to practice mindfulness to your emotions, you will want to turn your attention to the five components of emotion that we mentioned earlier. You will practice noticing and putting words onto:

Triggers: External or internal triggers that set off emotional reactions.

Thoughts: Including your core assumptions and interpretations about your emotions and the situation in which they occur.

Physical responses: How your body reacts with emotion, such as increased heart rate (anger), dry mouth (as with anxiety), clenched fists, body language, facial expressions and action urges that you experience.

Expression: What did you do or say that grew out of your emotional experience?

Emotional Fallout: What are the consequences of your chosen course of action? Have you set yourself up to feel the same emotion again?

MINDFULNESS TO EMOTION COMPONENTS

Notice your emotion: Allow yourself to be aware of what it is that you are feeling at the moment you feel it. Do not let your emotion pass without recognition.

See your emotion: Watch it coming and going, without holding onto it, and without avoiding it or shunning it.

Notice what triggered your emotion: Was it something someone said? Was it a thought or memory that came to mind? Were you tired, hungry or hurt?

Allow your awareness to expand to bodily sensations. What is your body doing? What is your face doing?

As you take action, let your awareness absorb what you are deciding to do. See your urges in your mind, and carefully and attentively watch your actions all the way through to the end of the sequence of events in this situation. Really KNOW what you are doing.

Label your emotion. Using descriptive and nonjudgmental language, say to yourself, "I notice a feeling of anger rising up inside of me," or "I can feel that the urge to run away and avoid is present." Do this without acting on your anger or your urge. Just **put words on what you are experiencing**. Describe factually the trigger for your emotion. Stay away from inflammatory and judgmental language that doesn't really tell you anything but about your judgments. Put words on your thoughts, labeling them as thoughts about the trigger, knowing that the trigger and your thoughts are not the same.

Describe the actions you take. Put words on the fallout of your actions that grow out of your emotions and your choice of actions. Of course, loving actions are easier to accept than angry, fearful or guilty ones.

Stay present. Once again, you are working at living a mindful life, part of which is staying put in the moment you are living, even a stressful moment, fully participating in your own life just as it is at that moment.

You will practice **noticing, describing and staying in the moment** of all five components of your emotional experiences.

Doing this over time will help you experience and stay connected to your primary emotional experiences as they happen, and eventually you will find yourself less encumbered by those complicated and messy secondary emotions.

We can't stress enough the importance and power of labeling your own emotional experiences in a manner that makes sense to you. This is critical to increasing emotional control. People who are able to label their emotional experiences, and therefore know what they are, typically show fairly good emotional control as well as impulse control.

It's not just a gift granted as a wish fulfilled by a genie. It is a skill that can be **learned** through **repeated practice**.

Somewhere in their histories, people with effective emotional control learned how to label their emotions, perhaps with the help of parents in an environment that wasn't rife with invalidation.

Now it is your time to learn.

Chapter X

SPECTRUMS OF EMOTIONS

We're offering you one more guide to aid in your practice just before you begin working on your emotion skills, notably mindfulness to emotion. Since emotions range in intensity, it can be helpful to have a few extra words in your verbal arsenal that might resonate with your experience. "Anger" may be too strong a word if you're feeling annoyed, or it might be too weak a word if you're feeling enraged.

As you work through your first worksheet, feel free to refer back to this emotion spectrum cheat sheet for ideas about words that match what you are feeling. You can certainly use others. This is just to help you widen your options if you happen to be at a loss for labels.

WORKSHEET:
EMOTION SPECTRUM *cheat sheet*

Happy/Joy:
content, cheerful, delighted, bubbly, euphoric, ecstatic

Fear/Anxiety:
nervous, careful, watchful, concerned, afraid, worried, paranoid

Love:
caring, fondness, affectionate, adoring, compassionate, kindness

Sadness:
bummed, disappointed, down, sad, gloomy, grieving, crushed

Interest:
interested, fascinated, attracted, magnetized, absorbed, enthralled

Guilt/Shame:
guilt, contrite, remorseful, discombobulated, shame, invalidated

Anger:
annoyed, upset, miffed, irritated, agitated, pissed, angry, rage

✏️ Exercise:
mindfulness to emotion: AWARENESS TO THE 5 COMPONENTS

To practice mindfulness to your emotions, use this worksheet, following it step by step as a way to record your practice noticing and labeling the five components of emotions. Summarize a recent emotional experience below. Try to do at least three of these for three separate days this week to get in some good basic practice.

Name/label the emotion:

....
....
....
....

Was this a primary or secondary emotional response?

Primary   Secondary   (circle)

....
....
....
....
....

Identify emotion triggers:

....
....
....
....
....

Identify thoughts (judgments, interpretations):

....
....
....
....

Identify physical responses (urges, posture, facial expression):

....
....
....
....

Emotion Expression (what did you do, say?):
....
....
....
....

Emotional Fallout (how are things for you, what other outcomes?):
....
....
....
....

Identify the function of your emotion:
....
....
....
....

✏️ Exercise:
mindfulness to emotion:
EMPHASIZING DESCRIBING

Use this worksheet to practice applying factual language to your emotional experiences. Make copies of this worksheet so that you can use it repeatedly since practice is required to increase skills. After you complete each item, go back and double-check for any judgmental language you may not have noticed before, and try to rephrase the description in factual terms. Draw from recent emotional experiences from today or within the last week or month.

Anger

Non-judgmentally describe an experience of anger:

....
....
....
....

Non-judgmentally describe your angry thoughts:

....
....
....
....

Anxiety

Non-judgmentally describe an experience of anxiety:

....
....
....
....

Non-judgmentally describe your anxious thoughts:

....
....
....
....

Fear

Non-judgmentally describe an experience of fear:
....
....
....
....
....

Non-judgmentally describe your fearful thoughts:
....
....
....
....

Sadness

Non-judgmentally describe an experience of sorrow/sadness:
....
....
....
....

Non-judgmentally describe your sad/sorrowful thoughts:
....
....
....
....

Guilt/Shame

Non-judgmentally describe an experience of guilt/shame:
....
....
....
....
....

Non-judgmentally describe your guilt/shame thoughts:
....
....
....
....

✏️ Exercise:
mindfulness to emotion: ASSESSING YOUR PRACTICE

Use this worksheet to evaluate your practice of noticing and labeling components of your emotions. This worksheet will help you to identify any potential obstacles that you may need to address to increase your effectiveness in this area. Keep at it.

If there is a particular emotion that is difficult to apply factual non-judgmental language to, especially as you experience the emotion, which one is it?

- **Anger**
- **Anxiety**
- **Fear**
- **Sadness/ Sorrow**
- **Guilt/Shame**

What is your guess as to why this particular emotion is more difficult than the others to apply non-judgmental language to? Is it due to any of the following?

- This is the emotion that I feel more strongly than the others when it's triggered
- This is the emotion I seem to feel more frequently than the others
- This emotion is one that was most reviled in my home when I was growing up
- I still have very strong habits of judging my emotional experiences
- Other: ....

Note the emotion that you have the most difficulty with, here, so you can think of new tactics to address it when you begin to work on changing your emotions:

....
....
....
....
....
....
....

✏️ Exercise:

mindfulness to emotion: DAILY SITUATIONS FOR NOTICING EMOTIONS

Use this worksheet as a guide for situations in which you can practice noticing and labeling your emotions. Check each box per situation that you practice this week, and write in the emotion that you **felt in that situation**.

Follow up with rating the effectiveness of your practice
Rating scale:
0 = none at all
1 = mild effectiveness
2 = slightly effective
3 = moderately effective
4 = very effective
5 = extremely effective).

☐ **At work today:**

Emotion: _____ Rate effectiveness practice (0 to 5): _____

☐ **With my family:**

Emotion: _____ Rate effectiveness practice (0 to 5): _____

☐ **Toward myself:**

Emotion: _____ Rate effectiveness practice (0 to 5): _____

☐ **Within my relationship with my significant other:**

Emotion: _____ Rate effectiveness practice (0 to 5): _____

Chapter XI

EMOTIONAL TOLERANCE

*Although this is the beginning of the chapter on increasing your **emotional tolerance**, you have already been practicing building your emotional tolerance, by observing and not reacting to (or terminating), your emotional experiences. You have already started to practice exposure strategies, gradually and increasingly exposing yourself more and more to your emotional experiences. You have been learning how to put words on these experiences, as your awareness to your emotions continues to grow.*

To increase your tolerance for your emotional experiences, you are going to need to experience emotions, which you will.

But you won't be sitting around waiting for something to stir you up; you're actually going to seek out and participate in situations that will require you to experience at least minimal discomfort, and maybe in some cases, great discomfort.

Remember from the early chapters, the bad news about DBT is that it doesn't *free* you from pain — since pain is inevitable. But the good news is it *can* help you end your emotional suffering leading you to a life guided by skillful living.

You will also work somewhat on your beliefs about emotions and how to challenge them.

The next chapter will be more narrowly focused on thinking patterns but as you know, these skills intersect and overlap with one another.

GENERAL GUIDELINES FOR INCREASING YOUR TOLERANCE FOR EMOTIONS:

- **Allow yourself to feel your emotion as it happens.** Allow the emotional experiences to happen, allowing also, yourself to feel it without judging it, escaping from the moment into fantasies about things you'd rather be doing, or ruminating on how unfair the situation is. Trying to escape or avoid your emotions will likely lead to secondary emotional experiences, ineffective actions, and you'll miss out on your chance to increase your tolerance for your emotions. Stay with it as long as you can. **Use your breathing** during this **exposure to your emotion** to assist you in tolerating strong emotions. If the emotions become too strong, just mindfully, not impulsively, set them aside and commit to allow yourself to feel your emotions when they are again triggered. Setting them aside mindfully is not a setback, nor a failure on your part. In fact, it is a triumph as you decisively and knowingly, with your full awareness, choose to set them aside, committing to come back to the practice. Because your emotions will return, you'll again have the chance to practice.

- **Don't prematurely terminate your emotion.** Continue this exposure to emotion as you **practice breathing** and **being mindful** to your emotions. Don't quickly or impulsively end the emotional experience. Don't interrupt the primary emotion with invalidating thoughts, dissociation, or by banishing them to an inner dark closet. Just sit with the emotion for a little bit longer than you want to, and then mindfully take a break, as described above. You will gradually push yourself to new limits of tolerance, feeling yourself becoming emotionally stronger.

- **Sit with your emotion for a moment, using mindfulness.** As you sit with your primary emotion, allowing yourself to experience it, use your mindfulness skills to fully observe and notice the experience with all its sensations, change in facial expression and body language. Let physical urges come into your awareness, and name the urge with factual, descriptive language, watching it as it comes and goes. The urge will soon subside, whatever it is.

- **Let go of the emotions.** Just as you let the emotion come as it's triggered, let it go as it wanes in its power. If you're experiencing negative emotions (anxiety, anger, sadness), don't tell yourself things such as "I deserve this," as though the negative emotion is some kind of deserved punishment. Don't try to keep the emotion around by ruminating on it, adding judgment or invalidating thoughts to it. You'll only risk secondary emotional responses and will delay the experience of the reality that **emotions don't last forever**, even if for a long while, and this is another **key to freedom** from your emotional suffering.

✏️ Exercise:
tolerating emotions:
BEGINNING PRACTICE

Describe your experience of allowing your emotional experience. What was it like?

....
....
....
....

Describe how you avoided quickly terminating the experience. If you reached a limit where you needed to mindfully set it aside, describe that practice.

....
....
....
....

Describe here your sitting with your emotions, and how you employed mindfulness. Include thoughts and feelings, negative and positive.

....
....
....
....

Describe how you practiced letting go of the emotions, including any difficulties doing so.

....
....
....
....

EXPOSURE TO EMOTIONS

To increase your tolerance to strong emotions, you need exposure to them to a level of mild to moderate discomfort while at the same time blocking any avoidance responses, including dissociation, ignoring, suppression or otherwise blunting your emotions.

As one of our DBT clients once asked, "How can I live with my anger ... until I start living with my anger?"

Permitting and tolerating emotional experiences is how you live with your emotions.

To practice exposure to emotion, and increase your tolerance for emotion, try to adhere to the following guidelines for an effective practice and for gains in tolerance:

1) Begin with information

2) Expose yourself to moderately emotional situations

3) Stay present

4) Block avoidant responses

In the coming week, commit yourself to approach situations that trigger at least moderately strong emotions that you find uncomfortable such as anger, fear and so forth.

Sometimes these situations will spring themselves upon you and will provide you with an opportunity to practice tolerating your emotions with your new skills.

Use the following worksheet to guide and record your practice. Use this worksheet to record your emotions, triggers, thoughts and urges to escape your emotions, including any avoidant or skillful behaviors you engaged in.

You will want to stay with the emotion just a little past the moment you think you need a break for maximum results.

✏ Exercise:
tolerating emotions: MORE EXPOSURE

Practice tolerating your emotions with your new skills. Describe your emotion and the skills used:

Monday
....
....
....

Tuesday
....
....
....

Wednesday
....
....
....

Thursday
....
....
....

Friday
....
....
....

Saturday
....
....
....

Sunday
....
....
....

INCREASING YOUR EMOTIONAL RESILIENCE

Additional Guidelines for Living an Emotionally-Effective Life:

Emotions are valid. Learning to give yourself permission to experience your emotions fully, and believing your emotions are true and valid, is part of the trick to having control over your emotional world.

Every time you feel your emotions becoming activated, tell yourself that your emotions are telling you something, or that they are helping to effectively propel you through your day. You don't have to have the permission of others to feel, since feeling is perfectly natural.

Keep fighting the old tapes of invalidation that will sometimes intrude. Use your mindfulness skills to be aware of these thoughts and use your other thinking skills to counter those thoughts.

Emotions are not facts. Your emotions are responses to events that are either internal or external, to you, and even though they're powerful; they are responses to something going on, your experience of them. Thoughts about emotions are not facts.

EMOTIONAL EXPRESSION VS. EMOTIONAL CONTROL: FINDING THE BALANCE

Exercising can also lead to increased awareness. Getting out and going for a walk oftentimes clears the mind so you can have insight to the different aspects of your emotional experiences.

For example, a very normal trigger might come up leading someone to start experiencing an emotion. They may tell themselves that they have no right to have that emotion and that emotion makes them a bad person.

It is similar to standing in the rain. Once you know and believe it is raining, you can choose to move out of the rain. It's the same principle when it comes to raining in your emotions: express what you feel, experience it internally, and then move on when you are ready, instead of letting the emotion control you. In other words, go for a walk. Or choose another activity.

Learn and understand what the eight primary emotions are, and then go through an example of each one. You will need to become familiar with experiencing a normal range of emotions. It is best to practice with someone you feel safe with, someone who will be supportive of your emotional experiences. It can be difficult to find someone who can tolerate expressions of anger, sadness, shame and fear.

However, they are perfectly normal, healthy emotions and are necessary for living life.

EFFECTS OF ABUSE

OVERVIEW OF EMOTIONAL SUFFERING

There are terrible things that have happened to people and emotionally they just can't be explained. The level of terror and the enduring pain that emotional suffering can deliver can understandably become unbearable. People who are veiled by misery have a tendency to live day after day, trying to just shrug off the pain and do the best that they can to avoid feeling their painful emotions. Perhaps surprisingly, it is this avoidance of emotion itself that can lead to a life of emotional suffering.

These extremes can create a lot of confusion for your family and friends who are trying to help. You may get accused of exaggerating or manipulating, instead of being seen as a person who truly needs help, understanding, support and love. People within your environment oftentimes become rejecting. Those around you no longer want to support the emotional needs that you have and often invalidate very real emotions. And you might find yourself invalidating very real emotions at times, and at other times flying off the handle, so to speak, over things that are very small, leaving you confused, as well.

The essential component of regulating your emotions is to validate what is real and work to act opposite to what is not. Doing "opposite emotion action" will be explained in greater detail in an upcoming chapter. You must give yourself permission to feel your emotions and be willing to accept them.

There are also internal and external causes for emotional triggers. For someone with BPD, the biosocial theory is used to explain the combination of symptoms that arise. I will try to break down this theory to help you make sense of your emotional extremes.

Biological

In DBT, the biosocial theory, based on a combination of biological and environmental factors, is offered as a frame for understanding the root causes of BPD.

It is when these two merge together in a heightened state that dysregulation can occur. Dysregulation simply means that a person starts to respond out of kilter. This can cause problems within all areas of life within their work/school performance, spiritual life, relationships with family and friends and with their emotional stability. In this section we are going to cover emotional stability.

However, there is a part of emotional instability that may be permanently present for you if you have a major affective disorder, such as any major mental illness like bipolar disorder, major depression, anxiety disorder, obsessive compulsive disorder, post-traumatic stress disorder, panic, agoraphobia and so on.

If you have a major affective disorder, you really need to seek help from a psychiatrist *and* a therapist to figure out how to find balance. Major affective disorders are just like any other physical illness. I often use diabetes as an example, because it is so similar.

When someone has a major affective disorder, they are going to have vulnerabilities in three areas.

The first is a heightened sensitivity to things that happen around them. When this happens, they are going to feel an extreme emotional reaction to it.
Oftentimes, people I have treated have said that they feel as if they are living through someone else. They can almost pick up exactly on what other people are
feeling and going through and it is very difficult for them to separate themselves from the other person or other events that are happening.

The second thing that happens is an extreme reaction. Once there is a heightened sensitivity, there is going to be an extreme emotional reaction.

The third thing is a slow return to baseline. It takes longer emotionally to return to feeling at ease. During the time it takes to return to feeling secure and comfortable, the emotional state is easily triggered and can rapidly escalate.

BIOLOGICAL FACTORS VS. SOCIAL FACTORS

The biosocial model is used to explain the development of Borderline Personality Disorder. This theory states that symptoms (emotional, behavioral, cognitive, interpersonal and self-dysregulation) develop and are maintained through an interaction of biological and social/learning factors. These factors lead to extremes in emotion and black and white thinking.

BIOLOGICAL FACTORS
Energy created by different feelings, such as happiness, anger, sadness, etc.

Emotional Vulnerability
A biological predisposition to:

1. High Sensitivity
- Immediate reactions to stimuli
- Low threshold for emotional reaction

2. High Reactivity
- Extreme reactions
- High arousal dysregulates cognitive processing

3. Slow Return to Baseline
- Long-lasting reactions
- Contributes to high sensitivity to next emotional stimulus

SOCIAL/LEARNING FACTORS
A learning environment that denies, ignores or minimizes a person's private emotional experiences.

An invalidating environment:

1. Indiscriminately rejects communication of private experiences and self-generated behaviors

2. Punishes emotional displays and intermittently reinforces emotional escalation

3. Over-simplifies ease of problem-solving and meeting goals

the take-away:
Biological factors and social/learning factors can intersect over time and lead to confusion about self, impulsivity, emotional instability and interpersonal problems.

Worksheet:
CHANGING EMOTIONS BY ACTING OPPOSITE TO THE CURRENT EMOTION

Fear

- Approach what you are afraid of doing ... AND DO IT.
- Aproach people and activities that scare you.
- Do things you feel pride in or that bring you a sense of accomplishment.
- Make a list of small steps toward a goal.

Guilt Or Shame (Justified)

- The emotion fits your wise mind values.
- Apologize and do something nice for a person you offended.
- Commit to avoiding that mistake in the future.
- Gracefully accept the consequences.
- **Let it go.**

Guilt Or Shame (Unjustified)

- The emotion does not fit your wise mind values.
- Continue to express and own your truth.
- Approach, don't avoid people or places that induce a feeling of shame. Be proud of yourself; let others own the shame.

Sadness Or Depression

- Get active and move. Walk the dog, jog, mow the grass, shoot hoops.
- Do things that make you feel awake and in charge.

Anger

- Rather than attack the person you are angry with, slowly move away.
- Avoid thinking about the anger you feel.
- Steer clear of rigid "I am always right" thinking.
- Do something nice rather than mean or spiteful.
- Try to feel empathy for the other person rather than blame.

Worksheet:
the interaction OF EMOTIONS, THOUGHTS AND BEHAVIORS

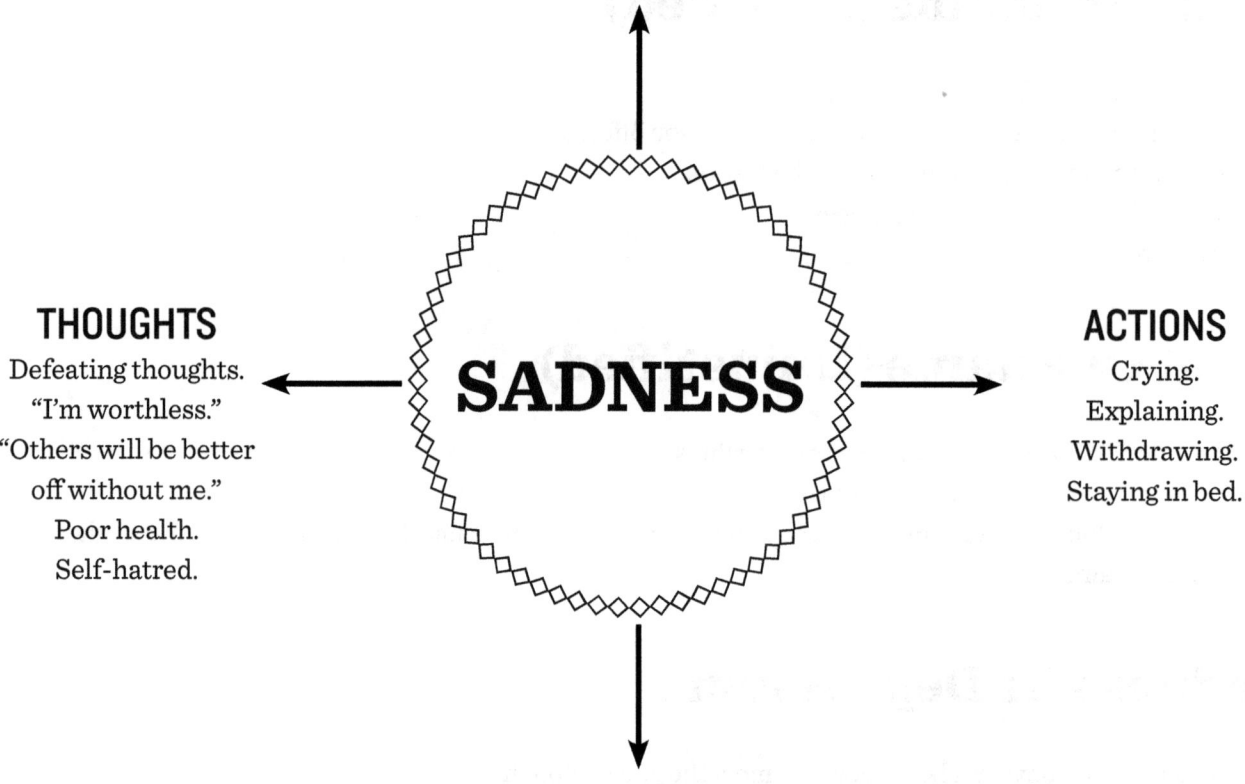

THE CAUSE
Rejection.
Believing the pain will never end.
Loss of something you love.
Being misunderstood.

THOUGHTS
Defeating thoughts.
"I'm worthless."
"Others will be better off without me."
Poor health.
Self-hatred.

SADNESS

ACTIONS
Crying.
Explaining.
Withdrawing.
Staying in bed.

BODY REACTIONS
No energy.
Walking and talking slow.
Head down.

Adapted from skills Training Manual for Treating Borderline Personality Disorder By Marsha Linehan. ©1993 The Guilford Press

Worksheet:
the interaction OF EMOTIONS, THOUGHTS AND BEHAVIORS

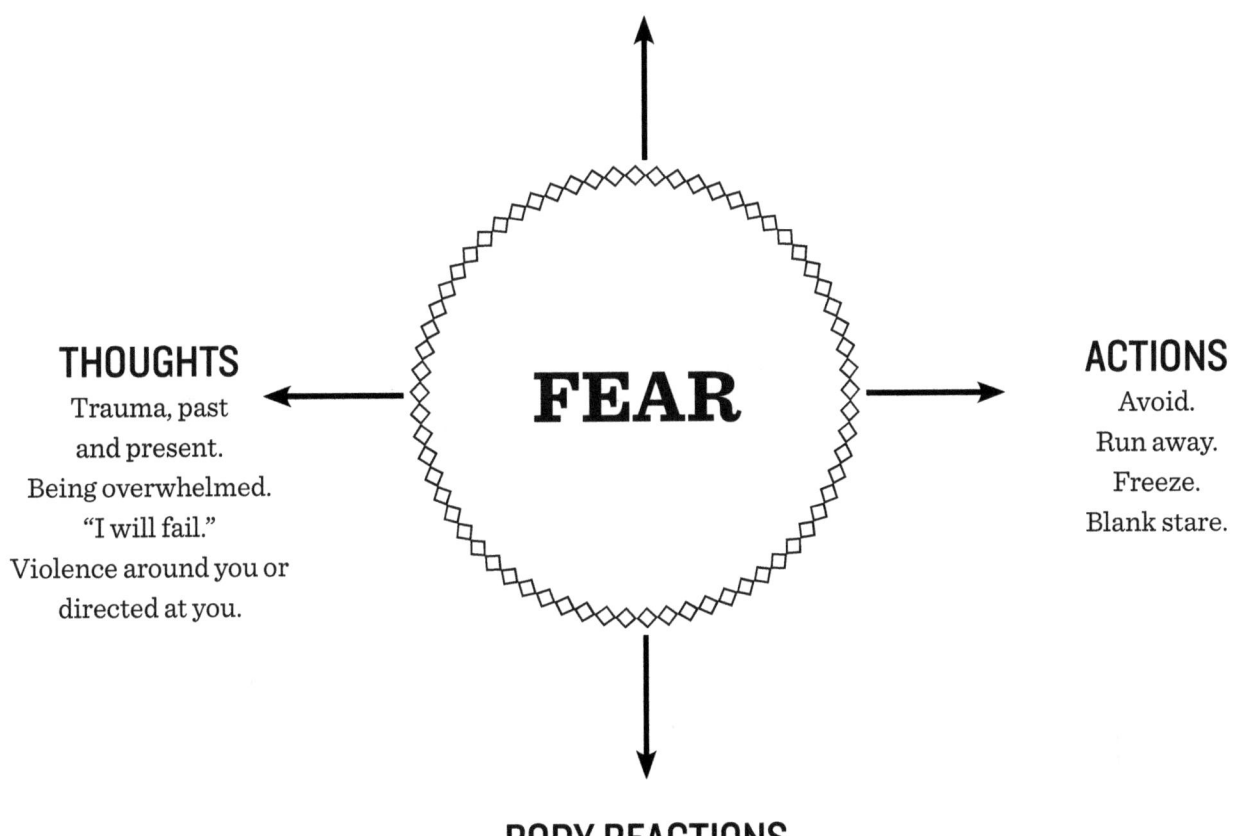

THE CAUSE
Being alone.
Thinking you are alone.
Being threatened.
Being in the dark.

THOUGHTS
Trauma, past and present.
Being overwhelmed.
"I will fail."
Violence around you or directed at you.

FEAR

ACTIONS
Avoid.
Run away.
Freeze.
Blank stare.

BODY REACTIONS
Sick to your stomach.
Lack of blood flow.
Hair stands on end.

Adapted from skills Training Manual for Treating Borderline Personality Disorder By Marsha Linehan. ©1993 The Guilford Press

Worksheet:
the interaction
OF EMOTIONS, THOUGHTS AND BEHAVIORS

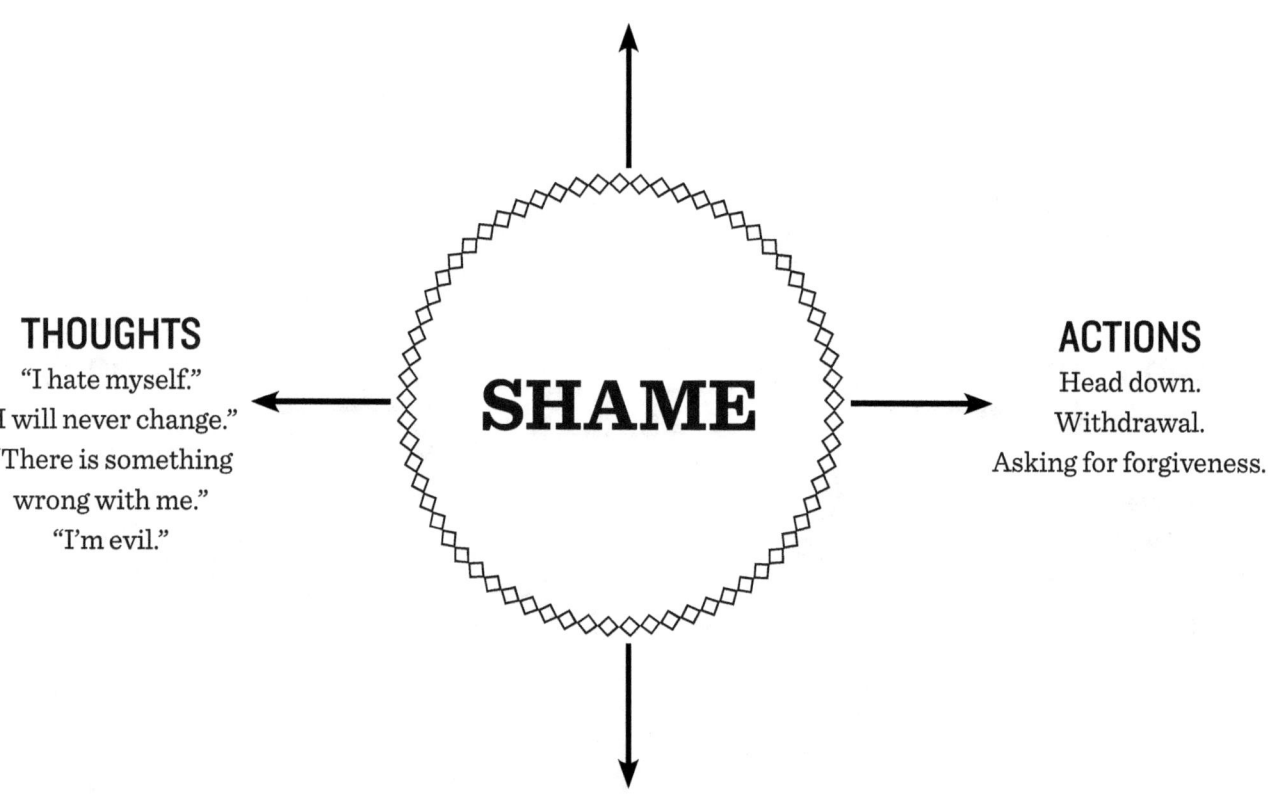

THE CAUSE
Abuse.
Betrayal by someone you love.
Rejection.

THOUGHTS
"I hate myself."
"I will never change."
"There is something wrong with me."
"I'm evil."

SHAME

ACTIONS
Head down.
Withdrawal.
Asking for forgiveness.

BODY REACTIONS
Obsessive thoughts about past mistakes.
Sick to stomach.
Crying.

Adapted from skills Training Manual for Treating Borderline Personality Disorder By Marsha Linehan. ©1993 The Guilford Press

Worksheet:
the interaction OF EMOTIONS, THOUGHTS AND BEHAVIORS

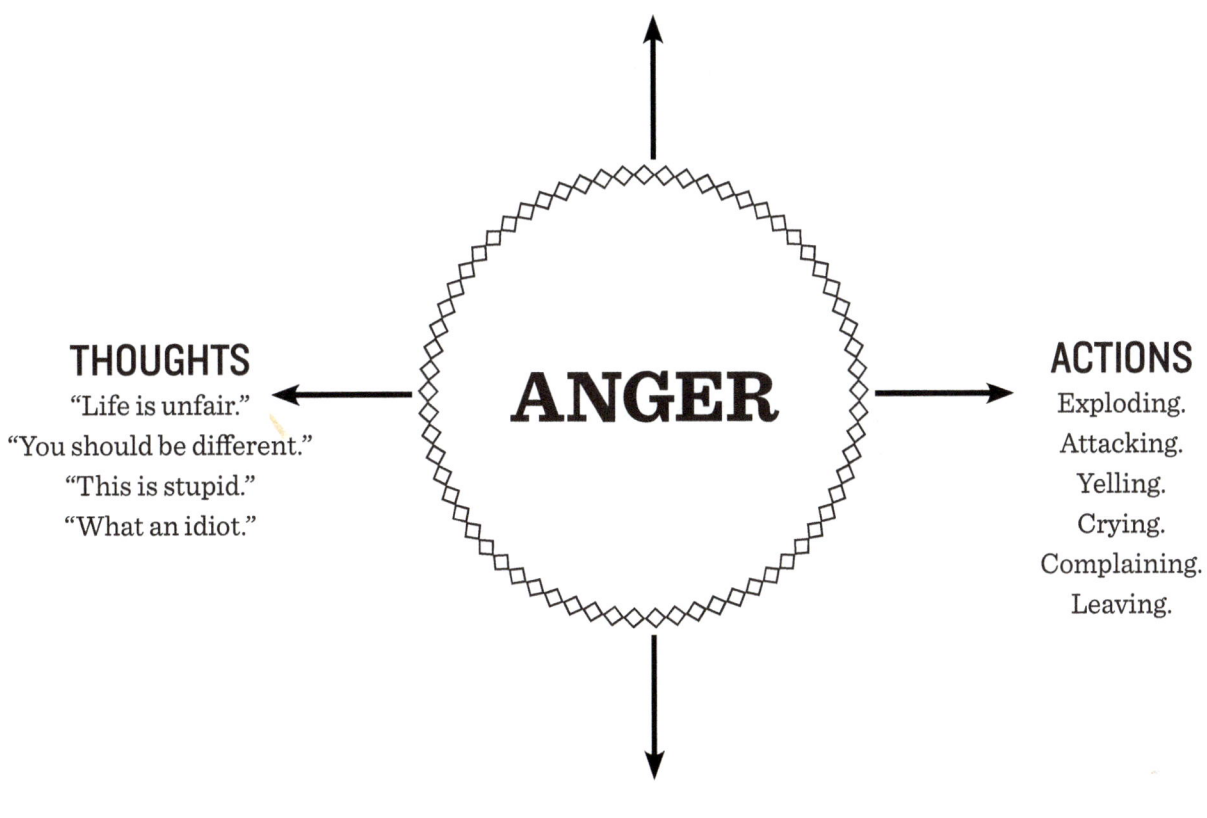

THE CAUSE
Physical pain.
Loss of something valuable.
Blocked from something you want.
Being threatened.
Believing you are being mistreated.

THOUGHTS
"Life is unfair."
"You should be different."
"This is stupid."
"What an idiot."

ANGER

ACTIONS
Exploding.
Attacking.
Yelling.
Crying.
Complaining.
Leaving.

BODY REACTIONS
Muscles tighten.
Glaring and staring.
Hot, red face.
Rush of adrenaline.

Adapted from skills Training Manual for Treating Borderline Personality Disorder By Marsha Linehan. ©1993 The Guilford Press

Worksheet:
the interaction OF EMOTIONS, THOUGHTS AND BEHAVIORS

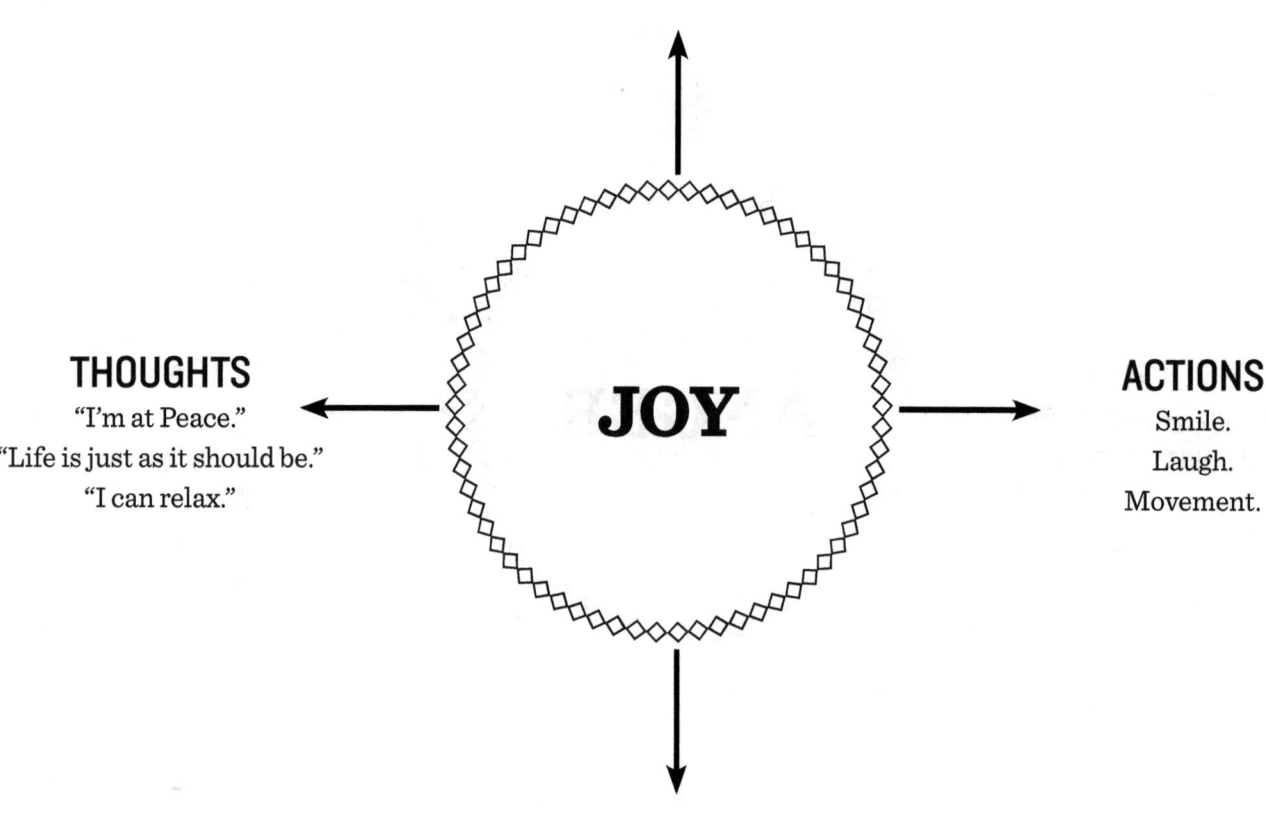

CAUSES
Success!
Accomplishing a task.
Working hard.
Learning.

THOUGHTS
"I'm at Peace."
"Life is just as it should be."
"I can relax."

JOY

ACTIONS
Smile.
Laugh.
Movement.

BODY REACTIONS
Energized.
Hyperactive.
Relaxed muscles.
Internal flame.

Adapted from skills Training Manual for Treating Borderline Personality Disorder By Marsha Linehan. ©1993 The Guilford Press

Chapter XII

FINDING YOUR PURPOSE

*Many people define their **purpose in life** by what they can provide to the world around them. Those who suffer from Borderline Personality Disorder often say that misery and pain are what they feel they have provided to the world around them. For this reason, it's easy to see how great degrees of misery and pain can take over.*

WHAT IS DISSOCIATION?

Dissociation is an extreme way of repressing your emotional feelings. This can be terrifying because it seems like an impossible task to control dissociation. However, it is important to note that some dissociation can be perfectly normal.

For instance, let's say you drive home from work the same way every day. One night, you get home from work and you don't remember driving home.

That would be an instance when you dissociated from driving. Dissociation becomes a problem when you repeatedly start to interact in life on autopilot; in other words, without truly being there.

Some people under extreme emotional stress forget arguments, forget acts of self-harm and don't even recall when they've seriously hurt others. The trance-like state that some people get into leads to a great deal of emotional turmoil later which leaves them feeling disconnected and hopeless.

When trauma occurs there may often be an injury to the brain which may be visible on brain scans as darkening in some areas. Therefore, it is conceivable that dissociation will eventually be linked to biological factors that start to happen after trauma.

For example, there has been documentation of post-traumatic stress disorder on individuals who fought in the Vietnam War. When these traumatic events are retriggered, there is often the tendency to dissociate and go into autopilot reactions. Post traumatic stress symptoms have been documented in the same way resulting from sexual abuse, assault and sever childhood abuse and neglect. The more frequent the dissociation is, and the longer that it occurs, the more disabled an individual can become.

OBSERVE AND CONQUER

Mastering the **skill of observing things** that are going on around you will help most in **combating dissociation.**

You must truly **tune into life** as it unfolds, staying in the present moment. Observe — internally — every single thought and feeling as it happens. Then observe, externally, all of your environmental surroundings. You should strive to stop and **smell the roses**, so to speak.

It is also important to fully understand the emotional reactivity that you have. This requires developing a comfortable approach with experiencing all emotions and staying present with them.

If you're someone who dissociates around anger, then you'll want to really pay attention to the emotional regulation component under anger and be able to stay present throughout the entire cycle of the emotion. The dissociation will not relieve the emotion: the emotion will continue to be there. It is only through honest expression of emotion, usually within a trusting, loving relationship, that you are able to release the emotion or even work through past traumas.

Past traumas *can* be worked through and dissociation *can* be limited.

However, to achieve this, you must **use skills to stay present** with your emotion and **honest within your relationships** and while expressing emotions.

BE PROACTIVE

We all want to be *proactive* in our lives instead of constantly *reacting* to the environment around us. To be proactive is to be able to **meet your goals** that you have set for yourself.

For people with Borderline Personality Disorder, being proactive becomes impossible if they are unable to regulate their emotions. Extreme emotional vulnerability — characterized by very high sensitivity to situations, then an extreme intense emotional reaction and a slow return to feeling normal again — typically leaves the person with Borderline Personality Disorder feeling out of control.

To **regulate your emotions** you must do four things.

First, you have to **inhibit inappropriate behavior** that results in the intense emotional response. In other words, when you get angry you have to be able to inhibit the urge to attack which comes from the emotion.

There may be many of you reading this who have been unable to inhibit your inappropriate emotional responses.

One lady once described the urge as being so overpowering that it was like firing off a gun, and that by the time she had the urge or realized she had the urge, the behavior was already done.

The second thing that you have to be able to do is to put **your emotions on the shelf**, so to speak. You must continue to pay attention to the task at hand and to meet the goals of your external environment.

Thirdly, you need to find an internal way to **self-soothe** and convince yourself that, ultimately, you will be ok, even though these emotions are occurring.

For individuals with Borderline Personality Disorder this usually means all emotions including love and joy as well as anger, fear, hurt and shame. Self-soothing requires an internal voice that provides comfort.

The fourth thing is that you must be able to **refocus your mental awareness** in the face of intense emotion. This act of refocusing allows you to be able to go back, if necessary, and explain yourself and your feeling with a greater presence of mind.

Therefore, to have a healthy structure by which to move forward, you develop ways to inhibit inappropriate behavior, continue to meet the needs of the external goals, self-soothe strong emotional urges and then keep focus when experiencing strong emotions.

I realize this may sound overwhelming, so I suggest breaking it down. You can use the following exercise to go through an ideal emotional response.

✏️ Exercise:

be emotionally proactive:
PLAN AHEAD TO BE ABLE TO COPE

Think about an upcoming event or situation that will trigger a strong emotional response. Use this excercise to plan ahead. Remember to keep your eyes on your objectives and to let go of any anger or need to prove you're right to anyone else.

What are some ways you will inhibit emotional responses? Ideally will you do or say:
....
....
....
....
....

Put your emotion on the shelf. What are some coping skills to pay attention to the task at hand?
....
....
....
....
....

What are some ways to remind yourself everything will be okay or ways you can self-soothe?
....
....
....
....
....

Outline your goal for the interaction if the trigger involves another person. Ignore others' attempts to distract you from your goal, including threats and put-downs.
....
....
....
....
....

HOW DO YOU TRUST IN YOUR OWN EMOTIONAL RESPONSES?

For many of you reading this book, being part of an environment that constantly invalidates your own reality has taught you to distrust yourself. This distrust can lead to a pattern of ambivalence within your personal relationships.

I would imagine that many of you reading this book have not been part of families where a) you can trust that when you express your emotions regarding hurt or pain that the other people will actually change their behaviors or b) others come to a realization that they do not want to hurt you and then take responsibility for the pain and the pattern of pain that continue on.

The invalidating environment continues on a path that tries to convince you that it was actually *you* who caused all the problems, created all the pain and who continues to be the source of all the conflict.

If you are a person who is involved in an invalidating environment, you may need additional help to sort out **what is valid and what is not valid**.

There are different environments that promote different types of invalidation.

There is a **nonresponsive environment** where it is common to have extreme consequences and uncommon to have private experiences which receive positive support and response. In these environments, there is constant failure to support individualism.

The positive qualities in emotions then would actually be seen as negative and criticized.

For instance, if you are a person who is a hard worker, even that could be twisted into something "wrong with you." In invalidating environments, personal attributes are viewed as negative and the constant criticism becomes overwhelming.

In some environments, overwhelming demands are placed on individuals and this can be followed with extreme punishments. If you are a person who is suffering or has suffered through physical, sexual and/or emotional abuse, you have experienced the effects of an extremely invalidating environment.

In our society, there is a strong value of **individualism**. Pulling yourself up by the bootstraps, having a lot of self-control and individual achievement are the goals. These perceptions can lead to invalidation in which negative emotions are seen as a weakness.

All of a sudden it is not okay to be sick, to have any personal problems or to struggle in any way. This also will lead to dysregulation of emotion making it harder for you to follow your own goals and dreams.

The paradox here is clear.

Within an environment where you want individual achievement, there also must be an environment where people can freely discuss problems, emotions, sensitivity, pain, sorrow, sadness, anger, fear and shame.

Chapter XIII

MAINTAINING HEALTHY RELATIONSHIPS

Maintaining healthy relationships, whether personal or professional, is a vital component to a fulfilling life for anyone. But healthy relationships do not magically happen overnight. Any successful relationship, whether with a family member, loved one, friend or co-worker, takes commitment, work and understanding. Solid relationships should be founded upon mutual respect, compromise and communication. But in order to have good relationships with others, it is essential to first have a good connection with yourself. This requires internal balance and strong self-respect and self-acceptance.

✏️ Exercise:

discover the future:
FIND HAPPINESS AND JOY

You have to look at things optimistically. Consider all that is possible. In the following exercise, you are going to find what is possible.

What have you been afraid to try in the past?
....
....
....
....

What were you afraid would happen if you tried?
....
....
....
....

If there were no obstacles, what would you choose to be doing right now?
....
....
....
....

Describe in detail what your plans for the future would hold.
....
....
....
....

What are the individual steps it would take to meet each one of those individual goals?
....
....
....
....

What are the first steps that you will need to take?
....
....
....
....

Are you afraid of succeeding?
....
....
....
....

What would you lose if you succeeded at meeting those goals?
....
....
....
....

What worrisome thoughts come to your mind when thinking of taking the first steps?
....
....
....
....

How can you stay in the moment and start acting opposite to those troublesome thoughts?
....
....
....
....

What are your hobbies and interests?
....
....
....
....

Make a list below of things that you might be interested in.
....
....
....
....

Are there any obstacles to pursuing your interests such as lack of support, fear of failure?
....
....
....
....

Below, you will create a list of some ways to overcome some of the obstacles.

What are your strengths and interests? List 10 items you see as your strengths.
....
....
....
....

Identify three other people who share the same strengths and interests as you.
....
....
....
....

Identify strengths and interests that any of your friends or family members have that you feel you do not have.
....
....
....
....

Identify the strengths and interests that you have that they do not have.
....
....
....
....

How do you feel about sharing your strengths with the other person?
....
....
....
....

Do you feel vulnerable or envious when your strengths do not overlap?
....
....
....
....

What are some things that you are clearly better at and how can you be vulnerable to their insecurities?
....
....
....
....

Identify some opportunities to share more deeply with your family and friends. People who have Borderline Personality Disorder frequently state that they do not know ***who they are***. This has developed due to years and years of constant compromise where they have given in to the wants and needs of others while trying to make a relationship work as well as trying to avoid the expression of painful emotions.

The avoidance of expressing painful emotions inevitably leads to a pattern of extremes. Constant avoidance and confrontation within the relationship and lack of defining your own set of values and beliefs is the underlying cause of the chaos.

Many people believe the myth that if you are willing to sacrifice your desires for another person, you'll be able to be fulfilled within the relationship. Therefore, the intent based on a false assumption destroys the relationship. To maintain the relationships, you must be willing to bring up conflict before it is overwhelming and define your values.

The old phrase "**you can't love another if you don't love yourself first**" definitely holds true.

So how do you find love for yourself? How do you define who you really are?

For most people this is a simple question. There is an inner voice that will answer when asked — ***if you listen***.

Usually a positive self-concept has been developed and this question only comes up in the face of intense struggle, change or pain.

For people with Borderline Personality Disorder, that is, in essence, everyday life. However, do not doubt for one minute that you are truly here, truly alive and you already are truly a whole person.

Defining who you are stems from having the faith that you already are a whole person, and knowing that **you are here for a reason** and that, ultimately, you cannot fail.

Try to view perceived failures as simply more opportunities for growth and learning. And remember, as long as you are alive, there is always hope. I hope that you will make a conscious effort to enjoy life and engage in the uncertain process of defining yourself through life experiences, your relationships and how you treat others.

Ultimately, you will have achieved the greatest thing in life: **the ability to love yourself**.

How to Create Healthy Relationships

So what is the secret to creating and keeping good relationships?

This is the million-dollar question that everyone is trying to find the answer to.

There are books written expressly on how to have good business relationships, how to find the best job, how to follow your dreams, how to have a good marriage.

In the big picture, it doesn't matter if you suffer from Borderline Personality Disorder or if you're a very successful entrepreneur.

Most of us lack the skills that it takes for nurturing good relationships.

Healthy relationships are created by taking risks — emotional risks, that is. For someone with Borderline Personality Disorder, this can be terrifying.

Typically, I hear stories evolving out of two extremes.

An example of one extreme would be when someone tells me that they cannot express painful emotions within relationships because they believe that "nobody wants to hear that" or that nobody wants to be around him or her if they are sad, angry or in a lot of pain.

The other extreme would be when someone interacts in relationships by *only* expressing anger, pain and sadness.

In this chapter we are going to discuss the overall picture of how to **get and keep good relationships**, and the magic ingredient so necessary for **effective interaction** within relationships.

A healthy relationship is one where you are **understood, loved and nurtured**.

You have an obligation to use your voice to foster communication. Often, great relationships are described as conversations you never want to end.

Many people were raised in environments that invalidated their personal experiences of the world around them. Therefore, the internal confusion of what is real and what is not real sets in and the communication is stifled.

I do not want to make light of the terribly abusive childhood some of you have experienced. Extreme abuse or a slight nuance of disapproval can stifle voices. Our body language, facial expressions and words are all used to relate to others. In extreme cases, people have learned to shut down all of their communication, including facial and body language, to ensure personal safety. If you can relate to this, or if others are clueless to how you really feel, this chapter will challenge you to openly express your thoughts, feelings and beliefs.

You will begin by redefining your current relationships, how you express emotions and typical avoidance patterns. Then you will address difficulties surrounding self-validation, finding balance and relying on others.

Finally, the role and effect of your mental illness and past suicide attempts will be explored. The following pages will instruct in the self-exploration of your relationships, with tools on how to create and repair relationships.

First you will need to define current relationships. In this section, honestly explore the types of relationships you currently hold.

Be nonjudgmental in your approach; that is, stick to the facts as much as you can and try not to harshly judge yourself for any relationships that are less than ideal.

Defining your relationships:

How long is a typical relationship for you?

....
....
....
....

Are there any common factors in the ways that your relationships end?

....
....
....
....

Types of relationships you have:

What type of relationships do you have? (Loving, nurturing, sexual, abusive)

....
....
....
....

When you're sad, are you able to communicate your feelings to the people in your relationships and ask for understanding?

....
....
....
....

Are you able to ask people for help with the little problems before they turn into a major crisis?

....
....
....
....

How much energy do you use thinking about and trying to meet the expectations of others?

....
....
....
....

Do you ever minimize to others the level of difficulty you had in accomplishing a task?

....
....
....
....

Reciprocity (or to reciprocate) is the balance of giving back equally what you get in a relationship. Are your relationships reciprocal? Is there balanced "give and take?"

....
....
....
....

Do you have, or have you had, healthy relationships which incorporate unconditional acceptance — honesty, kindness, love, nurturing?

....
....
....
....

In your relationships, do you ever find yourself in the role of the caregiver?

....
....
....
....

In your relationships, are you ever the one being taken care of?
....
....
....
....

Are you in that main role in all of your relationships?
....
....
....
....

What happens in your relationships when you experience intense emotions?

a. Is there an outburst or do you hide your emotions?
b. How does the person(s) deal with it?
c. If loving, kind or nurturing, do you accept it or push them away?
d. How could you deal with it differently?

EXPLORE YOUR FEARS

Developing healthy relationships is about finding balance and resolving conflicts before they become overwhelming. Mark the areas that need to be improved and then make a commitment to be willing to start using the relationship tools to improve the relationship.

Many people with BPD end relationships too soon, due to negative assumptions that they will not be understood. Resist the urge to end relationships prior to using skills to communicate your feelings and nurture the other person.

Fears of abandonment are common and lead to many of the negative assumptions individuals hold that stifle their healthy participation in relationships.

Following is an exercise to explore your fears of abandonment:

ABANDONMENT

Have you ever just left a relationship abruptly without a reason or cause?
....
....
....
....

Are you in or have you ever been in a relationship where the other person wanted out, but you couldn't let go?

....
....
....
....

Have you ever felt you don't need anyone in your life?

....
....
....
....

Does a crisis occur if someone else ends a relationship?

....
....
....
....

Have you ever thought your life would end if your special friendship/relationship were to end?

....
....
....
....

EXPRESSING YOUR EMOTIONS

What are your typical ways to express emotion? During this exercise you may want to share this with people you are in relationships with and get their feedback to the questions.

How do you express feelings?

....
....
....
....

How do you express your feelings in your relationships?

....
....
....
....

Do you ever hide your experiences to hide your feelings?

....
....
....
....

Do you ever get so overwhelmed with stress that your life becomes a series of crises even if just for a day or two?

....
....
....
....

OPEN DOORS INSTEAD OF CLOSING THEM

Avoidance will lead directly to confrontation. You must exercise caution when it comes to steering clear of conflict. Many people believe that if they let a conflict go that they will save the relationship. But letting pain and problems stew and gain momentum is precisely what may lead to the demise of a relationship.

I continually tell myself that if I choose to ignore a problem I am also choosing to end the relationship.

This may be a difficult concept to adhere to. However, be willing to engage and you will find exactly what you are looking for. The love and nurturing you desire will be possible to achieve if you **embrace life** and the challenges it brings to your door.

Use this exercise to explore your use of avoidance:

When overwhelmed with feelings do you showcase any atypical behaviors? (Examples include: drinking, drugs, binge eating, vomiting, fasting, cutting, burning, clawing, nail biting, arguing, fist fighting, driving fast, etc.)

....
....
....
....

Does being in new situations or trying new things (foods, crafts, etc.) cause mild anxiety, a lot of anxiety or sheer panic?

....
....
....
....

Have you ever (how many times) found yourself trying to find a way around things or situations in your relationships or do you take the blame even when you had nothing to do with the situation?
....
....
....
....

Do you take words, twist them by just one or two words to make it mean something totally different?
....
....
....
....

Do you ever use drugs and/or alcohol to go along with the people in your relationships when you really don't want to?
....
....
....
....

Do you use, or have you ever used self-harm as a way to release feelings?
....
....
....
....

If yes, what types of self-harm do you do?
....
....
....
....

What or how do you feel after self-harm is done?
....
....
....
....

Do you talk via the Internet, telephone or in person with anyone after you have done self-harm?

....
....
....
....

How do you explain the self-harm done to your body to the people in your relationships?

....
....
....
....

DO YOU ACCEPT YOURSELF?

Now you need to explore the relationship you have with yourself. This exercise will offer clues on where you need to do some work in accepting yourself and valuing your beliefs.

Important note: You will not be able to gain the respect of others without respecting yourself. Self harm or any self destructive behavior is not respecting yourself. Even if nobody knows, you can't deny the truth and your relationships will suffer.

- Do you validate yourself?
- Do you need people around you to make you feel valuable?
- What are your expectations of yourself?
- Is there a timeframe on your expectations?
- Do you have confidence in your own capabilities?
- Do you use your own experiences to help you through the tough times or do you require solutions from others?
- Do you ever hide your experiences to hide your feelings?
- Do you feel like you deserve to be punished by the people in relationships with you if you don't perform as high as their standards or higher?

FINDING INTERNAL BALANCE

Lastly, you need to find balance in your internal view and how you have fun. Here are a few questions on defining your involvement with spirituality and recreational activities.

Are you in balance?
- Do you have a spiritual belief?
- What kind of recreational activities do you do?
- Alone or with someone?

For those of you who have been in relationships where suicidal feelings have been a part of the intensity of your emotions, don't worry. Those feelings can be addressed honestly and worked through. You will want to be honest and direct, then reevaluate your involvement in the relationship. Suicidal feelings may return when in crisis. Make a safety plan and when these feelings return, follow the plan.

Are you pondering suicide?
....
....
....
....

Have you ever threatened suicide as a way to keep someone from ending a relationship?
....
....
....
....

3) Have you ever threatened or attempted to commit suicide?
....
....
....
....

Talk about the above responses with the person you love. Recommit to life and staying alive no matter the outcome of the conflict. Be sincere. You have caused turmoil and hurt that takes time to heal.

DEALING WITH STIGMAS

In this next section you will explore questions regarding the effect of your mental illness on your relationships. These questions are often overlooked due to the stigma associated with mental illness. Remember that your diagnosis is simply a set of symptoms that have been categorized and ultimately say little to nothing about who you truly are.

Make it a priority to strike up relationships with people who are willing to relate with you rather than simply label you.

Effects of your mental illness on your relationships:

Since being diagnosed with your illness, how have you and the people in your relationships tried to learn more?
....
....
....
....

Is your illness an open subject in your relationships or is it swept under the rug like a secret?
....
....
....
....

How do you feel about the people in your relationships knowing that you have a mental illness?
....
....
....
....

Do you ever feel like your value as a person has changed due to your mental illness diagnosis?
....
....
....
....

How do your family members or the other people in relationships with you feel about your illness (in your words)?
....
....
....
....

How do you feel about your illness?
....
....
....
....

What are your expectations of therapy?
....
....
....
....

Have you tried to hide or keep secret the fact that you have a mental illness?

....
....
....
....

Do you deny, question or accept the diagnosis you've been given?

....
....
....
....

How much information has actually been explained about your mental illness to you and your family members and the people in your relationships?

....
....
....
....

How do people treat you differently now as compared to before they knew you had a mental illness?

....
....
....
....

How do you feel having a mental illness will affect you in forming relationships in the future? With treatment?

....
....
....
....

With treatment what do you think will happen in your current relationships?

....
....
....
....

Honest communication with loved ones is the key to happiness. I hope you will find the courage to share your struggles and those around you find the courage to listen and support you. Remember to engage in the relationship, you must make the commitment to stay alive no matter what happens.

ACCEPTING ASSISTANCE & RELYING ON OTHERS

Now comes the challenging part; you must be willing to relate to and rely on others. You have to be willing to accept help and trust that others will be there for you.

Do you have a support system? Who (family, friends, any relationships) and what organizations do you use to help you through the hard times?

....
....
....
....

Do you have a supportive person you can call anytime, night or day, to help you through a rough time?

....
....
....
....

Is that person reliable and usually available?

....
....
....
....

4) Do you have a back-up person or place for times of crisis?

....
....
....
....

Cultivate the above relationships if they are lacking. Join social groups online, go to church, reach out to neighbors, pick a hobby and join a club, go to therapy. Engage with people through online support groups such as *mydbtgroup.com*.

Interpersonal Effectiveness Tools

Dialectical Behavior Therapy is about finding balance. And there is no other single area in which it is more important to find balance than in relationships.

Interpersonal effectiveness skills have to do with finding balance and reciprocity within your relationships. You also have to tend to the demands of life and resist the urge to migrate toward avoidance and confrontation.

People with Borderline Personality Disorder oftentimes swing between conflict avoidance and intense confrontation.

This is not much different than people without BPD; therefore this section becomes particularly challenging because you are going to be interacting with people nearer the avoidance and confrontation, and actually have secondary benefits and gains to maintaining a chaotic relationship style.

Becoming assertive and taking charge of your own life requires a lot of skill. However, just as in all dialectical dilemmas, you can go to one extreme where you believe you are responsible for all the interactions … or the other extreme where you don't take responsibility for anything.

But in the end, remember that ultimately the choice is yours.

The first step that we are going to discuss is how exactly you should attend to relationships. Anytime that you want to explore interpersonal effectiveness skills, you need to define what your objective is within the interaction.

Usually a person has three different objectives:

- The first is to obtain something that they want or to say "no" to something they don't want.
- The second is to keep a good relationship alive and to build upon that relationship.
- The third is to define your values and self-respect within the relationship.

GETTING WHAT YOU WANT OR SAYING "NO"

With the first objective, to obtain something you want or to say "no" to a request, you must stand up for yourself. Be your own advocate and ask for the things you need or want. This requires overcoming a lot of hurdles about asking in general.

SKILL FOR ASKING FOR SOMETHING OR SAYING "NO"

1) Describe exactly what you want, what you are responding to, or say "no" clearly. This needs to be done first thing. I am sure you can relate with the old familiar scenario of needing to discuss a conflict and instead dancing around the subject. That approach is not effective. You need to address the conflict immediately.

2) Second, give a short explanation of your feelings.

3) Reinforce the positive or negative consequences for not getting what you want.

An example:
I want you to use this exercise.
In my experience it has worked wonderfully.
You will find it improves your communication, too.

Keep in mind that you should do this exercise with confidence. Don't look down, mumble, apologize or do anything else that would give the receiver an impression that you are not serious. If you feel they are not receiving you message; repeat it over and over again.

Your goal is to be effective.

MAINTAINING GOOD RELATIONSHIPS

In the next area, you will need to be proactive when it comes to keeping and maintaining good relationships. Some relationships have a purpose yet are not close relationships — such as those with a boss or others in positions of authority.

Each one of these areas is going to have a specific set of tools to use in order to make the personal interaction more effective. I'm aware of a lot of people who have different phrases including:

"I'm not going to kiss up to anyone" that reduces their effectiveness.

You must be cautious when you define which tool to use that you are the most effective in using that tool. You must also keep in mind that **you cannot control situations** and therefore, no matter how effective you are, sometimes there is nothing you can do or say to cause the situation to be any different.

Many people with Borderline Personality Disorder get stuck in relationship ruts. They have difficulty maintaining good relationships because they let personal pain and problems build up over time.

People with BPD oftentimes carry around with them fears and myths about how to act in relationships, believing that it is best to keep negative feelings to themselves.

This is due to a longstanding pattern of invalidation within their environment. In other words, being told that they should just feel happy when they are not; buck up and deal with it, just "change your emotions."

These myths develop and are carried around, keeping individuals from confronting problems as they arise, believing instead that they should just let it go and try to find a way to be ok and deal with it.

Just to give you an idea of how people can feel, I often hear people say, "I create my own problems, its just in my head and I should just think differently."

Perhaps you have even thought these things yourself.

Other myths include believing that other people really do not care or that there is no use for negative emotions within relationships. Some people believe that if they make a request of someone else then that shows that he or she is a weak and vulnerable person. Others feel they need to say "yes" to everything, otherwise they must be a self-centered person. The list goes on.

It's easy to see how internal hurt and problems can build up until they culminate in a crisis situation leading to a verbal explosion, quiet avoidance or the inability to say "no."

BALANCE YOURSELF, BALANCE LIFE

When going through this section, you need to balance things that you want out of life and what you honestly feel entitled to receive.

This is why some people who are family and friends of people with Borderline Personality Disorder believe that they themselves have to walk on eggshells. They believe that someone with Borderline Personality Disorder is so dependent upon what they say or do that they really are restricted to not say or do anything.

So, in reality, not attending to small problems as they arise creates an environment of fear.

This can lead to everyone involved believing that if even a small conflict is brought up, it could lead to a drastic outcome.

The person with Borderline Personality Disorder can start to feel this detachment and it increases fear and anxiety and a need to go to extreme measures to keep the relationship.

It is important to start using everyday skills to really challenge negative expectations within relationships. Otherwise, these relationships will constantly be doomed.

Relationship skills must be used to head off problems before they arise.

SELF-RESPECT

The last section that you need to focus on is building self-respect and mastery over skills. This is where self-esteem is rooted.

The more that you are able to stand up for yourself, complete goals that you set for yourself and take advantages of opportunities that enable you to feel good about yourself, the more confident you will become.

It is critical to really work on balancing life **priorities and demands**.

And understand that balancing priorities and demands is a difficult skill for all of us to master.

Perhaps you are someone who is overwhelmed by all the demands that are placed on you, or maybe you are at the other end of the spectrum where nobody places any demands on you.

No matter where you fall on the line, to get a grip on your priorities and demands, you must first understand what priorities are, and subsequently, what *your* priorities are.

Simply put, priorities are what you hold to be valuable (most important).

✏ Exercise:
THINGS YOU HOLD TO BE VALUABLE VS. DEMANDS

Please make a list of all the things that you hold to be valuable. Then create a separate list of all the demands placed upon you.

If you find your list too short, feel free to add in some hopes and dreams of what you would like to be doing and ways to create more structure and responsibility and how you can offer to do things for others if your demands list is too short.

Use yourself as your own gauge. Try to resist the temptation of looking around and believing that you should be doing as much or as little as those around you. This information is about you and for you.

In balancing priorities and demands, you must learn the art of saying "no" when your priorities and demands get out of balance. Your other alternative is to reduce the number of priorities that are in your life.

The next step to achieving personal balance is to understand what you need in life and what you should do in life. A lot of self-care plays into this section. Balancing the "wants" and "shoulds" you have to do; in other words, the things you want to do and are required to do by others.

Worksheet:
BALANCING WANTS AND SHOULDS

I <u>want</u> to do this . . .

Read a book
Watch TV
Computer games
Go for a walk
Cook
Play sports

I <u>should</u> do this . . .

Clean house
Laundry
Buy food
Pay bills
Go to work
Return phone calls

YOU WANT THESE TO BE BALANCED.

Make a list of your wants and shoulds:

list your wants:

....
....
....
....
....

list your shoulds:

....
....
....
....
....

Do your wants and shoulds balance out?

MAINTAINING HEALTHY RELATIONSHIPS

Worksheet:
BUILDING MASTERY PRIORITIES VS. DEMANDS

Priorities are those things important to you; things that you want to do. Demands are those things other people want you to do. Most troubles with priorities and demands are due to your priorities competing with others' demands. Thus, you feel conflicted.

PRIORITIES	DEMANDS
These would be the big things in life that are most important to you.	These are some of the resposibilities or expectations that go along with priorities.
CHILDREN & FAMILY →	Spend quality time Feed them Discipline Praise Help them Take them places Hire childcare
WORK & MONEY →	Arrive on time Take verbal orders Clock in and out Be pleasant Meet deadlines Have transportation Engage in conversation
HOBBIES & INTERESTS →	Purchase items/Expense to do it Practice/Do it frequently Attend meetings/Get-togethers

the take-away:
Balancing priorities and demands is a necessary task for structuring one's life so that you fulfill your goals but still have some time to help others. This is difficult for everyone.

Worksheet:
REDUCING VULNERABILITY TO NEGATIVE EMOTIONS

Remember these skills with
"MEETS MASTERY"

MEDICATIONS - NO MOOD-ALTERING DRUGS
Take medications on time as prescribed. Avoid mood-altering drugs: Stay off non-prescribed drugs, including alcohol.

EAT - BALANCED DIET
Don't eat too much or too little. Stay away from foods that make you feel overly emotional.

EXERCISE - SWEAT IS GOOD FOR YOU!
Do some sort of exercise every day. Try to build up to 20 minutes of vigorous exercise daily.

TREATMENT - TREAT ANY PHYSICAL ILLNESSES
Take medications on time and as prescribed. Be aware of how you are feeling. Take care of your body. If you don't feel well, see a doctor.

SLEEP - GET THE RIGHT AMOUNT
Try to get a balanced amount of sleeping. Don't sleep too much nor too little. 7-9 hours of sleep a day is recommended.

the take-away:
Build mastery: Try to do one thing a day to make yourself feel competent and in control.

📄 Worksheet:
HOW TO ASK FOR SOMETHING EFFECTIVELY AND GET WHAT YOU WANT!

Remember these skills with **"SPEAK UP"**

STATE THE FACTS
Describe the situation. Stick to the facts. (What are you asking for?) Be very clear on what you want. "Would you like to go to a movie with me on Saturday?"

PAINT A VERBAL PICTURE
Express your feelings about the situation. "I feel (sad, mad, etc.) about the situation." Assume the other person will not know how you feel unless you tell them directly.

EXPRESS YOUR THOUGHTS AND FEELINGS
Assert yourself by asking for what you want or saying "NO" clearly. Remember the other person cannot read your mind. Say "I would like you to ... " Don't look down, be confident.

ASSERT YOURSELF AND BE CONFIDENT
Reward the other person ahead of time by explaining the positive effects of getting what you want. Think about how it would benefit the other person as well. Follow through with the reward.

KEEP FOCUSED ON YOUR MESSAGE
(Take hold of your mind) Keep your focus on what you want. Don't be distracted.

USE YOUR WORDS!
Use a confident tone of voice. Make good eye contact.

PICTURE THE RESULTS YOU WANT
Be willing to GIVE TO GET. Offer other solutions to a problem. Ask for others' input on how to solve the problem.

✏️ Exercise:
now, you do it.
PRACTICE USING THE "SPEAK UP" SKILL.

Describe the current situation. Tell the person exactly what you are reacting to. Stick to the facts.

....
....
....
....
....
....

Express your feelings and opinions about the situation. Assume that your feelings and opinions are not self-evident. Give a brief rationale. Use phrases such as "I want," "I don't want" instead of "I need," "You should," or "I can't."

....
....
....
....
....
....

Assert yourself by asking for what you want or saying "NO" clearly. Assume that others will not figure it out or do what you want unless you ask. Others cannot read your mind. Don't expect them to know how hard it is for you to ask directly for what you want.

....
....
....
....
....
....

Keep focused and reward the person ahead of time. Tell the person the positive effects of getting what you want or need. Tell him or her (if necessary) the negative effects of you not getting what you want or need. Help the person feel good ahead of time for doing or accepting what you want. Reward him or her afterward.

....
....
....
....
....
....

Worksheet:
HOW TO CULTIVATE A GOOD RELATIONSHIP

Remember these skills with **"RELAX"**

BE RATIONAL
Be reasonable and logical. Wait until you can approach calmly and rationally. Give yourself at least 24 hours before confronting a conflict. Take deep breaths and count to 10 if in a stressful situation. Keep in mind your goals for a situation and don't end relationships abruptly.

ENCOURAGE
Be interested and support those around you. Remember to give compliments and actively seek out more information regarding the other person.

LISTEN
Validate and acknowledge others' feelings. Practice repeating back what he or she is saying, giving your full attention to the conversation you are having in that very moment.

APPROVE OF THEIR INTERESTS
Be easy-going by smiling and laughing. Engage and try to enjoy the company of the other person, try not to rush or overly focus on yourself.

EXCUSE SHORTCOMINGS
Be easy-going and forgive others' mistakes. When emotions are running high, forgive quickly and move on.

✏️ Exercise:
now, you do it.
PRACTICE USING THE "RELAX" SKILL.

Practice these skills with a person special to you this week.

With whom did you choose to use the skill?
....
....
....
....
....

Did using the skill help you to improve your relationship with the person?
....
....
....
....
....

Which area was the most difficult for you to do?
....
....
....
....
....

What might you do differently next time to improve your use of the skill?
....
....
....
....
....

Worksheet:
HOW TO KEEP YOUR SELF-RESPECT

Remember these skills using **"WORTH"**

WALK TALL, TALK CONFIDENTLY
Look at others in the eye, don't apologize for yourself and be sure to treat yourself with the same kindness you give to others. No apologizing for being alive!

OPEN YOUR MIND
Try new experiences and be open to all observations. We perceive with our five senses, therefore pay close attention to your full awareness. Make a commitment to be a life-long learner and to constantly seek out self-awareness.

REALIZE YOUR WORTH
Learn what you value and don't change your beliefs to match others. State your opinions; share what you dream about and desire with others.

TRUST YOUR INSTINCTS
State your feelings and perceptions. Even if in the moment your feelings may seem out of place, talk it through and communicate the root cause of your thoughts and feelings.

HONOR PERSONAL VALUES AND PRINCIPLES
Don't lie, act helpless or exaggerate. Don't make up excuses.

✏️ Exercise:
now, you do it.
PRACTICE USING THE "WORTH" SKILL.

Practice these skills with a person special to you this week.

With whom did you choose to use the skill and in what situation?

....
....
....
....
....

Did using the skill help you gain more respect or feel more self-worth?

....
....
....
....
....

Which area was the most difficult for you to do?

....
....
....
....
....

What might you do differently next time to improve your use of the skill?

....
....
....
....
....

CONGRATS!

You have taken a major first step in turning your life around and dealing with any emotional difficulties that may be challenging you in your day-to-day life. By dedicating your time and energy to this workbook, you have already demonstrated a tremendous commitment to your mental well-being, and for that you should feel proud.

Whether you are suffering from Borderline Personality Disorder, a different diagnosis, or you simply want to escape a history of trauma and invalidation and regain control of your emotional self, you have taken a significant step in a positive direction.

In fact, mastering the skills presented in this workbook translates into a pathway to certain success for nearly anyone.

In the prior pages, you have learned about your emotions, including what exactly they are and what role they play in your life.

You have also learned through Dialectical Behavior Therapy how to employ the principles of **mindful living** to foster an environment conducive to self-understanding, self-respect and self-control. This, in turn, leads to improved relations in all areas of life, personally and professionally.

Most importantly, you have illustrated the fact that you have **hope** for a happier tomorrow. And with hope and a willingness to change negative thinking and self-defeating patterns of behavior, anything is possible.

I would not have created this workbook if I did not believe in the power of DBT.

But I have seen how this therapy can impact people's lives for the better; I have witnessed dramatic changes in my clients; and I have seen how integrating a new perspective can steer someone's life toward an infinitely-brighter path.

Every day, I am rewarded by the progress that my own clients make. Additionally, their actions, words and renewed passion for life further strengthen my belief in this therapy as well as my desire to assist as many people as I can.

I am proud of your efforts, as I know this is not an easy journey. But know that every step you take forward is leading you toward the life you want *and deserve*. Never lose faith in yourself and what you are capable of, for you are a tremendous gift to so many around you.

My challenge to you is to **start *now*** and ***move forward***. Utilize the problem-solving techniques presented in this workbook to bring a healthy balance to your thoughts, feelings and actions.

The **life of your dreams** *is right around the corner ... just waiting for you. Seize it!*

References

Astrachan-Fletcher, Ellan, and Maslar, Michael. 2009. *The Dialectical Behavior Therapy Skills Workbook for Bulimia*. Oakland, CA: New Harbinger Publications, Inc.

Dryden, Windy, and Raymond DiGiuseppe. 1990. *A Primer on Rational-Emotive Therapy*. Champaign, IL: Research Press.

Ellis, Albert. 1994. *Reason and Emotion in Psychotherapy*. New York: Birch Press Lane.

Harvey, Pat, and Penzo, Jeanine. 2009. *Parenting a Child Who Has Intense Emotions*. Oakland, CA: New Harbinger Publications, Inc.

Goleman, Daniel. 1995. *Emotional Intelligence*. New York: Bantam.

Gottman, John, and Nan Silver. 1994. *Why Marriages Succeed or Fail*. New York: Fireside.
1999. *The Seven Principles for Making Marriage Work*. New York: Three Rivers Press.

Greenberg, Leslie, and Susan M. Johnson. 1988. *Emotionally Focused Therapy for Couples*. New York: Guilford.

Greenberg, Leslie, and Sandra Paivio. 1997. *Working with Emotions in Psychotherapy*. New York: Guilford Press.

Kabat-Zinn, Jon. 1994. *Wherever You Go, There You Are*. New York: Hyperion.

Lazarus, Richard. 1991. *Emotion and Adaptation*. New York: Oxford University Press.

Linehan, Marsha. 1993a. *Cognitive-Behavioral Treatment of Borderline Personality Disorder*.
New York: Guilford.
1993b. *Skills Training Manual for Treating Borderline Personality Disorder*. New York: Guilford.

Gottman, John. 1997. *Raising an Emotionally Intelligent Child*. New York: Fireside.

Greenberg, Leslie, and J. Pascual-Leone. 1995. "A dialectical constructivist approach to experiential change." In Robert Neimeyer and Michael Mahoney, *Constructivism in Psychotherapy*. Washington, D.C.: APA Press.

Izard, Carroll. 1977. *Human Emotions*. New York: Plenum 1991. The Psychology of Emotions. New York: Plenum

Jacobson, Edmund. 1967. *The Biology of Emotions*. Springfield, IL: Charles C. Thomas

Kovecses, Zoltan. 1990. *Emotion Concepts*. New York: Springer-Verlag.

Lazarus, Richard, and Bernice Lazarus. 1994. *Passion and Reason: Making Sense of Our Emotions*. Washington, D.C.: APA Press

Niedenthal, Paula, and Shinobu Kitayama, eds. 1994. *The Heart's Eye: Emotional Influence in Perception and Attention*. San Diego: Academic Press.

Spradlin, Scott. 2003. *Don't Let Your Emotions Run Your Life*. Oakland, CA: New Harbinger Publications, Inc.

Strongman, Ken. 1996. *The Psychology of Emotion: Theories of Emotion in Perspective*. New York: John Wiley.

Tomkins, Silvan, and Carroll Izard, eds. 1965. *Affect, Cognition, and Personality* (4th ed.). New York: Springer Publishing.

Traue, Harald, and James Pennebakes, eds. 1993. *Emotion, Inhibition, and Health*. Gottingen, Germany: Hogrefe & Huber

Van Dijk, Sheri. 2009. *The Dialectical Behavior Therapy Skills Workbook for Bipolar Disorder*. Oakland, CA: New Harbinger Publications, Inc.

www.ingramcontent.com/pod-product-compliance
Lightning Source LLC
Chambersburg PA
CBHW080554090426

42735CB00016B/3238